DEGREES EAST
THE MAKING OF THE UNIVERSITY
OF EAST LONDON
1892–1992

Degrees East

The Making of the University of East London 1892-1992

TYRRELL BURGESS MICHAEL LOCKE
JOHN PRATT & NICK RICHARDS

ATHLONE
London & Atlantic Highlands, N.J.

First published 1995 by
THE ATHLONE PRESS LTD
1 Park Drive, London NW11 7SG
and 165 First Avenue,
Atlantic Highlands, NJ 07716

British Library Cataloguing in Publication Data
A catalogue record for this book is available
from the British Library

ISBN 0 485 11434 8   hb
0 485 12092 5   pb

Library of Congress Cataloging-in-Publication Data
Degrees East: The Making of the University of East London
1892–1992 / Tyrrell Burgess ... [et al.].
     p.   cm.
Includes bibliographical references and index.
ISBN 0-485-11434-8. -- ISBN 0-485-12092-5 (pbk.)
   1. Education. Higher--England--London--History--19th century.
2. Education, Higher--England--London--History--20th century.
3. East End (London, England)   I. Burgess, Tyrrell.
LA639.L8L43   1995
378.421--dc20   94-46791
                                                          CIP

Typeset by
Bibloset

Printed and bound in Great Britain by
the University Press, Cambridge

Contents

Introduction by the Vice-Chancellor, Professor Frank Gould

It may seem strange that the University of East London, one of the UK's new universities, should be writing an account of itself only three years after acquiring its new title. We are in fact an institution with a long and enterprising history, from our beginnings in 1898 as the West Ham Technical Institute, through the foundation in 1936 of the South East Essex Technical College, now our Barking Campus, to the marriage of the two institutions and what is now Waltham Forest College as the North East London Polytechnic in 1970, and up to the present day.

Until I read the text of this history I had not realised quite how complex and intriguing were the moves that led to the establishment of our predecessor institutions, nor how well these exemplify the radical developments which were taking place in British further and higher education throughout the twentieth century. At every stage of the evolution of the present university its staff and governors seem to have been at the centre of educational innovation and change, often with those at the highest levels of Government taking almost as lively an interest in our progress as our founding fathers in the local boroughs.

Today's students, like their predecessors, come in considerable numbers from the six London boroughs closest to us, and now include people from all over Greater London, from elsewhere in the UK, and from more than 70 countries throughout the world. But, as the reader will discover, the mission of the University of East London remains constant to its original vision, and the intentions of the institutions' founders are no less relevant and inspirational today than they were when this history began.

Acknowledgements

This book was commissioned by the University of East London as part of the work of the Centre for Institutional Studies. We have been grateful to the then Rector, Professor Gerald Fowler, and for the support of the present Vice-Chancellor, Professor Frank Gould and all our colleagues. We wish to record that in planning and writing the history of our own institution we have had enviable editorial independence.

We also spoke to a number of people formerly involved with the university or its constituent colleges, to whom we owe a special debt for their willingness to talk to us about the institution. What they said has greatly influenced what we have written but they are not, of course, responsible for our conclusions. They included Dr N.T. Bloomer, Councillor G.A. Brooker, Dr George Brosan, Dr Gerald Bulmer, A.F.G. Edwards, J.B. Fuller, Sir Norman Lindop, John Morris, Eric Robinson, Naomi Sargant and Sir Toby Weaver.

In addition, we would like to thank the keepers of the local studies collections of the London Boroughs of Newham, Waltham Forest and Barking & Dagenham, for giving us access to their archives.

CHAPTER 1

The University of East London, 1992

When the University of East London was designated by the Privy Council in June 1992 it already had an institutional history of over 100 years. During that time the problems of higher education – problems of numbers, governance, standards, level of work, purpose and funding – received many different solutions in universities, polytechnics and colleges. No institution had a richer experience of these various solutions that the University of East London. Its history thus embodies the changes, controversies and dilemmas of British higher education.

The University is now an independent corporation: its constituent colleges grew from two bursts of civic enterprise at Stratford and Dagenham. It was thereafter maintained by the local authorities until the gradual transition to central funding, which began in the 1970s, was completed in 1988. Its academic work has been in both the autonomous and the service traditions, and it has both suffered and resisted 'academic drift' from one to the other. Its students have at various times taken the degrees of the University of London and of the Council for National Academic Awards. In the years after 1970 it was a leading force in the establishment of a distinct idea of a 'polytechnic'. It has seen many versions of relationship with its hinterland and sought to take advantage of its dispersal over a wide area. Now, the University can be seen as a continuing solution to educational, social and economic problems. What were the characteristics of the institution that attained university status in 1992?

THE BARKING CAMPUS
The University is a 'dispersed institution', with one site in one east London borough and several in another. The Barking campus is in Longbridge Road, Dagenham, on the edge of the vast Becontree housing estate. The 1992 prospectus described it as 'set in a green field site, surrounded by trees and playing fields', though recent building programmes have stretched this romantic description to the limits of credibility.

Longbridge Road is dominated by the frontage of the original main building: the H-shaped South East Essex Technical College, designed in the 1930s by J Stuart, the Essex county architect. It was officially described as being 'in the Georgian tradition, the main object being to give an impression of lightness, strength and simplicity' (SEETC, 1936). Pevsner praised it faintly as 'symmetrical, large, with two somewhat projecting wings. The centre with a solid stone cupola. Three-storeyed, pale brick, quite an acceptable design' (Pevsner, 1954).

Above the main entrance, and on the first floor window balconies at the front of each wing, are inscribed the names of '...the famous men of science and letters from the earliest times down to the present day' (SEETC, 1936), including Einstein, Da Vinci, Rubens, Mill, Cavendish and Brunel. Around the upper part of the exterior walls a number of carved relief panels depict the industrious individual, engaged in pursuits considered appropriate by those who first commissioned the college: art or engineering, plastering or couture, commerce or needlework. A man conquers electricity with his bare hands. A naked woman studies botany. Others ice-skate, leap hurdles, play cricket.

Inside, the long corridors, high classrooms and (recent) cream paint celebrate a 1930s vision of education, and the sub-deco entrance hall announces that a sense of grandeur is not excluded. A huge hall rises through two storeys; above this is an echoing refectory the length of two cricket pitches. Housed in this main building are academic departments of law, economics, education and computing, together with the bursary, the academic registry and a conference centre. The rear of the building (which closes the H and creates a long quadrangle) was an early victim of financial cuts, and was reduced to a single storey when the college first opened. It had to wait until 1955 before another two storeys were added (SEETC, 1955). The quadrangle, though grassed and shrub fringed, is seldom used, except by a duck which for some years now has raised broods of ducklings there. The young birds stay, pampered by secretaries, until they are big enough to fly out.

Other buildings, later additions from different periods, are clustered around the old college, and an anonymous low slung engineering building lurks close behind. The names of the University's buildings tend to commemorate local worthies, powerful local government figures, prominent industrialists and businessmen who have served on the governing body. The psychology department once secured accommodation in a new building at Stratford through a timely proposal to name it after the then chairman. None of the buildings has been given or endowed by individuals or corporations.

The Frank Lampitt building is connected to the original block by a covered but draughty aerial walkway. It is a serious-looking structure, of

reinforced concrete wall panels which are of exposed
Mendip stone aggregate facing, each weighing approximately 16 tons, suspended from the roof structure and
tied back to the floors. (NELP, 1978)

The building was opened in 1978 and houses the largest
of the University libraries, covering science and technology, social sciences, arts and the humanities. It has been
estimated that on a busy day students borrow or return
a book every 12.7 seconds (PEL, 1992). This library was
home after 1971 to the internationally acclaimed Science
Fiction Foundation library collection, which moved to
Liverpool University in 1993. On the ground floor, below
the library, is the department of land surveying.

To the west of the main building stands the no-nonsense
engineering block, officially opened in 1966, when it was
claimed, optimistically, that

although the building is not in the same style as the original, harmony is achieved utilising materials of similar
colours and textures where possible. (BRCT, 1966)

The George Brooker building of 1991 has even less of
an air of reassuring permanence. It was constructed using
some of the most modern building techniques: the walls of
steel sandwich construction were manufactured in York,
and transported to the site for erection. Conception to
completion was speedy. External painting is in architects' beige or desert drab. Inside are cultural studies
and sociology, as well as the University's best equipped
lecture theatre.

The sports field, tennis courts, football field, and all
weather surface have been moved by an £8 million
building project, which has given the University its first
on-campus student residential accommodation: 504 student rooms, with laundry and facilities for the disabled.

The first of these new student halls of residence, Shepherd Hall, was formally opened on September 21st, 1992. It accommodated 144 students, enjoying all the benefits and teething troubles of a new facility.

Large areas of the site have been laid out to offer parking for 850 vehicles, and to avoid congestion on Campus access roads a 'red route' has been established. Any vehicle parked along the roadway marked with a single red line, risks being wheel-clamped, and its owner fined £10 by the University.

Among the other facilities at the Barking campus are a bookshop, student union shop and offices, music centre, two bars, and a nursery. The international headquarters of the Hydrographic Society also has an office here. The sports centre is open to the public, as part of a policy of integration with the local community.

THE STRATFORD CAMPUS

There is much less of a campus at Stratford: the University's sites are widely dispersed. Fortunately they are reasonably served by public transport. Most of the campus buildings are within a few minutes' walk of Stratford's shopping precinct. The most distinctive of all is the old West Ham Technical Institute, a grade II listed building at the corner of Romford Road and Water Lane, first opened in 1898. It contains the science faculty, and may be regarded as the seat of University government, as the Vice-Chancellor has his office there. The two and a half acre site also includes the Stratford public library and the Passmore Edwards Museum, both of which are owned by the London Borough of Newham, yet are integral to the University building. Pevsner described this in the following terms:

> Every conceivable motif is used which was available at that particular moment in the history of English architecture, when the allegiance to forms of the past was

at last thrown to the winds. Giant columns and Gibbs surrounds of windows are still permitted, but the turret and cupola shapes for instance are without any period precedent. Besides the grouping of masses is completely free. The college front is towards Romford Road, a symmetrical composition with two flanking turrets. The museum projects on the right, a lower domed block, and the Water Lane library recedes, ending in a turret of odd and playful shape. Altogether the architects have certainly enjoyed being fanciful and have not minded being a little vulgar. But the whole is of a robust vitality which seems enviable today.

The old Municipal College is of red brick with plenty of stone work, the exterior sculpture by W Binnie Rhind. The plentiful long trailing out tendrils and scrolls are especially characteristic of the 90s. Inside, the principal rooms are the Great Hall (80ft by 40ft, with a fibrous plaster ceiling) and the public lending library. (Pevsner, 1954)

Legend has it that the Technical Institute was built on a piece of ground once known as Stratford Common or 'Gallows Green'. Here, it has been said, the feudal Lord of the Manor, Sir Richard de Montfichet, erected a gibbet

for the purpose of wreaking vengeance on those who should be so unwise as to run counter to his lordly will....Instead of giving his tenants useful instruction and food for their minds in the shape of culture and knowledge, he gave them plenty of rope for their necks. (WHTI, 1898)

Behind the old technical institute, and across the road, is The Green. Originally the site of a territorial army barracks, it is now dominated by a large, solid, concrete clad block – the Arthur Edwards Building, completed in

1982 and opened by Sir Harold Wilson. Sheltering in its lee are garden shed laboratories (converted stables) with radiation hazard warnings on the doors. The earliest radiation suite on this site, first opened in the 1960s, was initially housed in a World War II bunker. More of the 'men (and women) in white coats' can be found here – psychologists, physiotherapists, and other boffins. A computer centre services the Campus.

Nearby, the bland Artillery Houses house student services, counsellors and University medical staff. By contrast, the nineteenth century St Helen's House on Water Lane offers a little pastoral relief, quaint, almost Tyrolean. It was originally established as a women's settlement in 1896. The other University buildings close behind appear to have stolen most of St Helen's garden while her back was turned.

In term time a constant trickle of academic humanity crosses the minor road, which separates The Green from the old Technical Institute, confounding short-cutting traffic. A redevelopment plan of the 1970s, to block the road off and turn it into a pedestrian precinct, remains unfulfilled (NELP, 1976).

A recent innocuous addition, just across the road from the old Technical Institute, is the Water Lane building, accommodating payroll, personnel and Management Information Services, and it is suitably discreet, except for a pair of embarrassed garden centre lions, cemented above the door entrance. At the other end of Water Lane, in Manbey Park Road, stands Maryland House, a former washhouse, and later depository, which contains the largest library on the Stratford campus, for science and psychology. The Centre for Institutional Studies is here, as is the Innovation Studies department, the campus office of the student union and a large bar which features regular entertainment.

Duncan House, on the dual carriageway towards the

Bow flyover, used to house the *Stratford Express*. It is the only University building in the western hemisphere, standing just beyond a bronze plate in the pavement marking the Greenwich Meridian. Approval for its 'refurbishment' in the 1970s was interpreted as stripping it down to the steel frame and rebuilding. When it was re-opened, the building was named after an early member of the staff at the West Ham Technical Institute, whose physics text book became a standard for generations of British students. It now houses the East London Business School, the University's business faculty.

A few minutes walk from Plaistow Underground Station, tucked out of sight of the main road and surrounded by cramped terraced houses, the Holbrook Centre is a typical late Victorian three decker board school building, with separate entrances for boys and girls and playground lavatories, still in use but heated. It is now largely the domain of architects, but there is also a small friendly library. It was once the temple of polytechnic unorthodoxy, the School for Independent Study.

The most remote outpost of the University, in truth just a bus ride away from Stratford shopping centre, must be Greengate House, Plaistow. A tall attractive, white bricked building, complete with Art Nouveau detail, it was built as a hostel for the YMCA, dedicated as a local war memorial, and opened in the presence of King George V and Queen Mary in 1921 (LBN, 1974). There is a broken backed swimming pool in the basement. The University's art and design school occupies the entire building: inside, a specialist library, two tired vestibule lifts, a warren of cranky rooms and work spaces which occasionally hold surprises – is it a broken locker or is it art?

Eventually it is the University's intention to vacate Holbrook and Greengate, as part of plans to centralise the Stratford Campus. In the short term some art and

design activities are being moved to Holbrook, allowing the creation of gallery and lecture theatre space at
Greengate.

There are two main sites for student accommodation
in Newham: part of the Woodlands Estate near West
Ham station, consisting of 45 four bedroomed apartments
currently owned by the Borough, and awaiting transfer
of ownership to the University, and the Park Village
accommodation in the north-western most corner of
the borough. The latter consists of two 12 storey tower
blocks and a number of houses, offering accommodation for over 500 students. Situated as they are, on
an isolated site behind Stratford railway yards and the
international freight terminal, the upper floors of the
tower blocks offer a commanding view of the site of
London's future Channel link. It could be a train spot-
ters' paradise. At Park Village, the University also has
nomination rights for a percentage of vacancies at the
Clays Lane Housing Co-operative. The Student Union's
Handbook has described this area as a 'groovy, partying
estate' (UELSU, 1989).

DOCKLANDS CAMPUS
In 1992 the University's annual report signalled an increas-
ing commitment to a new, third campus in the Royal
Docks 'as part of the development of the East Thames cor-
ridor'. It reported discussions with the London Docklands
Development Corporation and the Higher Education
Funding Council and promised that the University would
make a bid at the appropriate time:

> We see this as a logical development of both our
> involvement in the region and our central geographical
> location within it. It is, however, a £60 – £80 million
> project and there is much ground work to be done.
> (UEL, 1992)

STUDENTS

The business of a university is learning, whether by students, on the course provided, or by staff, in research, consultancy and educational development. On the whole this learning is organised round bodies of knowledge – disciplines or subjects – which together form a university's academic structure.

Reflecting the University's mission statement, its students (like those at many former polytechnics) are rather different, in character, background and interests, from the stereotypical 18 to 21 year olds of much university literature. In the academic year 1991-92 there were 9419 enrolled students. Of these over 55 per cent were on full-time courses, and 30 per cent on part-time and day and evening courses. In May 1990 roughly 45 per cent of part-time day and evening students lived in the outer east London boroughs. Many of them were local people. In October 1991, almost a third (31 per cent) of the full-time UK students were funded by the east London LEAs; Barking & Dagenham, Hackney, Havering, Newham, Redbridge, Tower Hamlets and Waltham Forest.

In 1990, 66 per cent of all students were aged 21 or over, and 44 per cent were aged 25 or over. In the University's nearest academic neighbour, Queen Mary and Westfield College in Stepney, the percentage of mature undergraduate students in 1991 was 13. (ACU, 1991).

On the ethnic origins of students, in May 1992, the largest groups were: white 47.4 per cent; Black African, 7.6 per cent; Indian, 7.1 per cent; Black Caribbean, 5.8 per cent. In 1990-1991 the balance between male and female students was fairly even: 51.7 per cent male to 48.3 per cent female. In October 1991 overseas students from 82 separate countries accounted for roughly 10 per cent of the full-time student population.

The University provides a range of services and facilities to support these students. With the opening in 1992 of an extended nursery for children at the Barking campus, the University is able to claim more childcare places than any comparable institution in the country. Two additional posts have been created in the Careers and the Counselling and Advisory Services to identify and meet specific needs of black students. The Careers Services takes pride in statistics suggesting that the employment rate for the University's graduates and diplomates is better than that of most other former polytechnics in London.

Membership fees and usage charges have been introduced in the sports centre. As a consequence, perhaps, use has greatly increased. Certainly they have made possible a continuing programme of improvement and redecoration in the centre, the opening of an extended and extremely popular fitness centre, the refurbishment of changing rooms, and major improvements to the communal areas. The Music Centre offers tuition and practice facilities to students. A choral group perform regularly, and lunchtime and evening recitals attract good audiences.

There is a flourishing Students' Union. One of its functions is to represent students on course committees and the Governing Body. All Union posts are elective through cross-campus ballots. There are no lectures coinciding with the Union's regular general meetings. The Students' Union also provides services. It has bars at both campuses, as well as shops and coffee bars. The entertainments the Union provides mainly take place in the bars and include discos, cabaret and small bands. The Union's magazine, *Overdraft*, is produced fortnightly and is distributed free of charge. It has been reviewed well on Radio 4, and recently one of its reporters was runner-up Student Journalist of the Year. The Union also provides free to first-year students a handbook on the University, London, and, as it says, 'lots more!'

The Union has many links with community organisations and cultural groups, and has arranged deals with local businesses, sports centres and so on. It funds and assists all the competitive inter-college sports teams. Areas of excellence in recent years have been football, netball and basketball. Non-competitive sports, including sub-aqua, canoeing, parascending and mountaineering, are also on offer.

Cultural societies are 'as varied as the imagination of the students, since it is they who set them up.' There are political groups, musical societies, international societies and course-based societies. Then of course there's RAG – raising money for charity – 'in loads of wild and wacky ways!' The Union also provides help with everyday welfare: inquiries about housing, grants and student loans, legal advice and debt counselling. It takes up complaints about courses or lecturers and advises students who fail.

ACADEMIC DEVELOPMENTS

The University employs well over 1,000 people, half of whom are academics. The academic staff work in five faculties, covering broad fields of study: the faculties of Design and the Built Environment, Social Sciences, Technology, the East London Business School and Science and Health. The University thus offers all the main academic disciplines except medicine, and all have distinguishing characteristics.

A common interest in Europe has characterised recent developments in the Faculty of Design and the Built Environment. There is an MSc in International Property Management and an MA in European Architectural Studies. Architecture students have recently won a prize for the best major project design in the Royal Institute of British Architects President's Medals for architecture in education. Christine Hawley, when head of architecture, won third prize in the competition for the design of the new European landmark of the World Trade Centre in Berlin. The School of Art and Design's Artist in Residency programme has been further developed by the creation of a postgraduate degree in art education. Land Surveying has successfully instituted an academic link programme with Bulgaria, and have joined Delft University and others on a Tempus project for Land Information Management in the restructuring of the economy in Eastern Europe. Estate Management has completed a study of business activity and land use patterns in the East Thames Corridor. The instruments used to measure distances in the javelin, discus, high jump and long jump at the Barcelona Olympics in 1992 were calibrated by staff from the departments of Land Surveying and Mathematical and Physical Sciences.

The East London Business School has been well represented overseas, with staff pursuing academic developments in Belgium Cyprus, France, Germany, Holland, Hong Kong, Malaysia, Nigeria, Russia, Singapore, Thailand and the United States. In addition to many reciprocal visits, the School has received academic colleagues from Greece, and Norway. The School was particularly delighted by the academic successes of several of its Singapore-based MBA students, who achieved distinctions.

Recent developments in the Institute of Health and Rehabilitation include masters programmes in health promotion and in physiotherapy, a postgraduate diploma in orthopaedic physiotherapy and health option in the combined studies degree. The Institute has collaborated with other institutes developing a diploma in professional studies in nursing at the Romford College of Nursing, Midwifery and Health Studies and a DipHE in Midwifery at the Romford College. Another development is the 'top-up' degree programme for staff who hold a number of different diploma qualifications in a range of professions which are allied to medicine and the programme will be taught on a multiprofessional basis.

In the Faculty of Science, the Department of Environmental Sciences examines the relationship between humankind and the environment, with special reference to the problems that have resulted directly from human activities. It offers honours degree courses in environmental sciences, environmental studies, wildlife conservation, animal biology, applied ecology, life sciences and archaeological sciences. Bananas, coconuts and date palms flourish in the laboratories.

The principal areas of interest of the Environment and Industry Research Unit have been in soil microboes, interactions between invertebrates, plants and micro-organisms, and biotransformations in semi-natural and disturbed ecosystems. This work has led to the development of a three dimensional ordination model of soil ecosystems based on size, composition and activity of the microbial community. The classification of systems and comparison of disturbed soils can help to enhance their rate of restoration. There is also an active programme investigating waste treatment using micro-organisms.

The Paleobiology Research Unit seeks to define and resolve problems concerning extinct organisms. It specializes in analytical studies of pollen and other remains of plants that lived up to 100 million years ago. Present projects aim to compare the geological ages of different sediments and try to establish an archive database of extinct plants. Its laboratory has recently analyzed 5000 year old beer from Egypt. Its work involves the construction of very large databases, and the Plant Fossil Record is an international computer archive, a database of all extinct plants. A working prototype containing more than 10,000 fossil plant genera records has been developed, and an associated database records the place and age of extinct plant occurrences. The Unit has many millions of records, and it can reconstruct the ecology, helping to predict climatic change and further extinctions. These activities are challenging traditional methods of study and use informatics at an international level. No longer are obscure bits of information just hidden on dusty top shelves in unknown libraries; the data are openly accessible to specialists and non-specialists alike. The Unit enjoys responding within minutes to a search request from, say, Florida to its 85MB database, and hopes that these changes may be in time to help to rescue the natural environment from destruction.

Since the political changes in eastern Europe the Unit has hosted working visits from palaeontologists in Germany, Poland, the Czech Republic and Romania. More than £200,000 has been awarded from EU funds for young scientists to work at the University learning new ways in which environmental problems can be better understood and resolved. A NATO sponsored workshop in November 1993 heard Russian, north American and European specialists in Tertiary plant palaeoecology, in order to advance theories of environmental change, in particular in relation to climates in the Arctic.

In addition to the activities of these units, the Department of Environmental Sciences has research activity in parasitology, ecology, archaeological sciences and the application of computers to biology. Most of these involve external collaborations both in Britain and in other parts of Europe.

The Department of Life Sciences was established in 1992 to accommodate existing work in microbiology and genetics, physiology and pharmacology, and biochemistry. The sandwich course for a degree on applied biology was the first ever course in biology to be validated by the CNAA in March 1964. Now, nearly thirty years on, the degree is still flourishing with an intake of over 100, nine named degree pathways, and a separate part-time degree with an additional five named pathways.

One of the studies in the Chemotherapy Research Unit (CRU), established in 1974, is of drugs which when chemically changed by tumour cells only, produce a highly toxic agent for less than a hundredth of a second.

This agent can kill tumour cells but does not last long enough to diffuse out of the cells and begin to damage normal cells. The CRU determines how the toxic agent damages the cells' genetic material and how efficiently the cell can recognise and repair the damage. This study has been funded by the Cancer Research Campaign and the Wellcome Trust.

Another study concerns the mechanism of drug resistance in a bacterium which is responsible for causing stomach and duodenal ulcers. Funded by the British Society for Antimicrobial Chemotherapy it involves collecting specimens of the bacterium from ulcer biopsies in patients from the UK, Europe and the USA. It analyses the protein catalysts of the bacterium to determine if they have mutated and whether the change could explain the resistance observed clinically.

The Psychology Department has had a reputation for very good teaching for many years but perhaps the most significant thing about it is the impact of its research in society. This is best represented by the Department's work on eyewitness testimony which has advanced courtroom practice and contributed to changes in legislation. The Department has also produced work on bias in television news which has shown, among other things, that bias is in the eye of the beholder as much as in the broadcast. Recent books written by members of the Department include work on health psychology, children and television, families and ethnicity and the second edition of its best selling introductory textbook of psychology.

The Faculty of Social Sciences is the fastest growing in the University. The main subject areas on which the faculty is based – law, economics, sociology, cultural studies, education and languages – are all areas of active student demand, and it has been possible both to expand existing degree programmes, and to develop new subject combinations and options to meet new student interests.

Among specific new course developments started recently
has been a new joint degree programme in social sciences, combining the subject areas of law, economics and
sociology.

The Department of Education and Community Studies has renewed its innovative teacher education programmes, including the initial training of graduates, based
in schools, in partnership with the London Borough of
Newham, and has developed a modular Masters programme in Professional Practice in Education, Institutional Studies and Voluntary Sector Studies. The Department of Economics has collaborated with the Department
of Economic Studies at Leeds University to produce
a new journal, *International Papers in Political Economy*.

Gardening is not usually associated with universities,
but it is the most popular outdoor leisure activity in the
country. According to the Mintel Report there are 20
million gardeners, 10 million of them enthusiastic about
it. On the Communications degree Martin Hoyles has
designed a unique course unit, based on his recent book
The Story of Gardening. It studies the political and social
history of gardening and its place in contemporary culture.
Students do a placement, for example in a public parks
department or allotment society.

The faculty's work also has an increasingly European
emphasis. Three Departments are already involved in
exchanges of students and staff through the European Community's ERASMUS scheme. Links have also been developed between two Departments and universities in Russia,
the Czech Republic, Slovakia, and in other countries of
Eastern Europe. Academic visits for lecturing and research
purposes from colleagues in other European countries are a
regular aspect of faculty life, and involve increasing numbers
of exchange students. The relocation of the language
service in the faculty and the University's proximity to
new European communication links gives this additional

emphasis. The newly launched BA in New Technology with European Studies recruited well to its target intake.

In the Faculty of Technology, recent new courses include computer and control engineering, product design, and an information technology minor. A novel work-based mode of study has been developed by the Department of Manufacturing Engineering and Design in partnership with the Ford Motor Company. Engineers based in Ford plants at Aveley and Dagenham who possess (typically) HNC or HND qualifications have been accepted on to the BEng Manufacturing Systems Engineering with advanced standing; their work experience and training courses have been evaluated using the credit accumulation and transfer scheme. After completing a specially designed bridging studies programme, students have sufficient credits to enter the final year of the degree. Because almost one half of this final year can be undertaken as part of their job at Ford, it is possible for these engineers to study the UEL based modules of the course part-time and complete their degree within one calendar year following the bridging studies programme. Over 60 engineers are currently studying on the scheme.

Research activities have continued to expand with the award of an SERC grant in electrical and electronic engineering, and the invitation of a member of staff to a visiting professorship in power engineering at Tokyo University. British Telecom have funded a post-doctoral research programme. There is a £3/4 million SERC/DTI/LINK research programme with a consortium of industrial companies, water companies and research institutions.

The University's degree scheme provides a flexible network of about 400 course units arranged within distinct subject areas (25 operated in 1992) from which students may select broad programmes of study suited to their needs and subject interests. In this way they may choose to follow single theme (specialised) degrees, joint honours degrees, combined subject degrees or degrees by independent study either full time or part time. Most of the 300 in the first year were mature students, many gaining admission on the basis of a mixture of educational qualifications and uncertified prior experience. The University has established firm links with a number of access programmes in colleges within east London, Essex and the east Thames region.

A major innovation of the former Polytechnic, independent study, now operates on a faculty basis. It is an integral element of the modularised system for flexible delivery of programmes and is available at diploma, degree and post-graduate level.

The University is committed to widening participation in its courses. The Access, Advice and Learning Development Unit has been involved with the North East London Access Federation and the Essex Access Consortium, and new links are developing with colleges within the London Open College Federation (LOCF) and the Kent Access Consortium, in anticipation of the development of the East Thames Corridor. It has organised, with Newham's Women's Unit and Newham Community College, an education and training fair for Asian Women. Its open days for access and mature students in October attract more than 800 visitors. It has been recognised as one of eight institutes providing particularly interesting models of access co-ordination. The Unit has developed the assessment of prior experiential learning. The advice required for assessing specific learning outcomes is a focus of links with local employers. It has also co-ordinated and integrated language and learning support within the University. Recent developments have included a 'diagnostic pack' to identify learning development needs, a referral procedure for students with learning and language difficulties, open learning resource centres at both campuses, safety net support to students, and support for black students with learning difficulties arising from cultural differences. A student guide to materials for interactive learning skills has been developed.

Like other institutions, the University takes pains to cultivate its links with schools and colleges. Since 1992 it has had a full-time schools and colleges liaison officer. Special emphasis has been placed on maintaining and developing links with schools in the local community. A project funded through the London East Training and Enterprise Council, local authorities and the University provides a route into higher education for young people in the local boroughs who have not achieved the academic grades of which they are capable.

The recruitment of students is an international and highly competitive activity. The University recruits from 72 countries worldwide and generates £3.5 million income a year from this source. Numbers of students from overseas are generally increasing, and particularly important have been links with Hong Kong, Malaysia, Israel, Sri Lanka, Nigeria and Cyprus. More recent links have been made with India, Pakistan and Korea. The University participates in many European ventures. Under the ERASMUS programme (European Action Scheme for the Mobility of University Students) there are ten programmes and exchanges have taken place with six EU countries. Under the TEMPUS scheme (Trans European Mobility Programme for University Studies) there are programmes in nurse education, electrical and electronic engineering and land surveying, mainly for training and consultancy with Poland, Hungary, the Czech Republic and Slovakia.

RESEARCH FUNDING

In recent years the University has made significant developments in its research capabilities. The amount of external income won as research grants exceeds £1 million, and, together with that obtained through consultancy and contract research has reached nearly £2 million. The increase in research income has been matched by increases in the number of research publications, research projects and research students. The University now houses nine research units.

A noticeable trend is the increased amount of research being carried out with collaborators in other institutions in the UK, in the rest of Europe and overseas, often with funds provided by the European Community. Over the last year new research links have been forged with the Czech Republic, Russia and many European Union countries. Collaborative research is now carried out with 54 institutions outside the UK and about 190 in it.

COMPUTING

The Computer Centre provides central resources for academic computing within the University. This has been revolutionised in the past two years, moving from a system based on Prime minicomputers and serial connections, to one based on personal workstations accessing an integrated University-wide network. The University-wide network is in turn connected to the rest of the UK academic community and the world beyond via JANET (the Joint Academic Network). Because of its high JANET usage, UEL has been selected as one of only four former polytechnics as a pilot site for the 'SuperJanet' project.

The full range of network facilities is also extended to the students. Every student who enrols at the University has disk space on a server, and has access to word processing software, laser and colour printers, electronic mail, programming languages, spreadsheets and databases, as well as to specialist departmental software. Students can use these from the Computer Centre's open access laboratories, or in departmental facilities connected to the network.

The Computer Centre has been able to provide and improve its services by devoting time to research and development. It aims to be a centre of excellence for computing within the University. Current projects include the 'SuperJanet' pilot, and investigating the technologies of networked Multi-Media that are expected to form the basis of new teaching methods for the next century.

LIBRARY AND OTHER SERVICES

The use of the Library is growing dramatically. A computerised system links all site libraries and gives complete access to holdings throughout the University, and it frees professional staff from clerical duties, to concentrate on responding to students and staff. The information technology resource centres at Maryland House and Barking are important components in the University's aim to move to open-learning, and there are sophisticated computer-based teaching facilities in all lecture theatres. All students are offered an appropriate course in information skills, and most students receive this in their first weeks at the University, its content being determined with their course tutors.

The Docklands and East Thames Unit was established in January 1992 to involve the University in the educational, social, cultural and economic regeneration of Docklands and the East Thames Corridor. Local large employers, LDDC, local councils and MPs have voiced support for a higher education campus as part of this regeneration, and the University's strategic plan a commits it to significant presence in Docklands. The Unit has been working with the faculty deans and other staff to develop proposals for a Docklands campus. The Unit also participates in the Stratford and Lea Valley Economic Regeneration Forum and the Stratford City Challenge programme, for which the University's Centre for Institutional Studies provides the evaluation team.

The University has received £1 million over five years from the Department of Employment for its part in the Enterprise in Higher Education (EHE) initiative. This is intended to develop higher education through mutually agreed and contracted processes of curriculum change. The main aims of the University's programme are to encourage students to take greater responsibility for their own learning, and to create an environment in which students, the institution and employers or practitioners work together. The programme has already presented the institution with such diverse innovations as proposals for a new degree in partnership with the Ford Motor Company Limited, the development of a student record of achievement, a mentoring scheme for black students, and a taped prospectus, as well as examples of the way courses can be changed to enable students to plan, monitor and review their own learning. Motivation and ownership have been the key themes for staff development in 'enterprise'. The new University-wide programme, *Focusing on the Learner*, responds to individual needs and promotes seminars, workshops and conferences. The Enterprise Unit has held a national conference jointly with the Royal Society of Arts Higher Education for Capability scheme on using learning contracts in higher education.

The University's commitment to equal opportunities has been strengthened in recent years. Services for students with disabilities and special needs have been developed: there are over 100 students with varying needs in this group. Progress has been made in capital provision, equipment, a staff development video, a 'talking prospectus' and in a considerable amount of support given to individuals on applications, post-entry assistance and design of appropriate assessments. Targets and performance indicators have been developed to encourage positive action for under-represented groups, particularly women, members of ethnic minorities, and people with disabilities. Procedures for dealing with complaints of discrimination and harassment are being developed.

GOVERNANCE

Under the Articles of Government the academic affairs of
the University are in the hands of the Academic Board. It is
responsible for research, scholarship, teaching and courses.
It determines the criteria for the admission of students,
for their assessment and examination. It approves the
content of the curriculum, maintains academic standards
and arranges for the validation and review of courses. It
appoints internal and external examiners and determines
procedures for the award and qualification of honorary
academic titles. It advises the vice-chancellor on academic
development and the resources needed to support it. Much
of the work of the academic board is done through
committees, for example for validation, research, teaching
and learning, enterprise and ethics. In 1992 the University's
'quality assurance' system was radically revised, involving
an academic planning committee with faculty boards and
faculty validation and review sub-committees. The new
system emphasises the annual review of courses. In 1992
the academic board also agreed to convert existing first
degree and diploma courses into a 'modular form' and to
deliver them on a 'semester' basis. The chief executive of
the university is the vice-chancellor (in 1993, Professor
Frank Gould) who is advised by a Board of Management
consisting of senior officers.

The University is a 'higher education corporation', the
members of which are the University's board of governors.
The governors determine the educational character and
mission of the University and oversee its activities. They
are responsible for the effective and efficient use of
resources, for the solvency of the institution and for
safeguarding its assets: they approve annual estimates.
They appoint senior officers of the University and set
the framework for the pay and conditions of staff.

The University costs well over forty million pounds
a year to run. Half of its income comes from public

funds, through the Higher Education Funding Council for England, a third from student fees and the rest from other fees and charges. The University has no endowment income. Under half its expenditure is on academic departments, a quarter on administration, central and other support departments, a fifth on 'other costs' and about a tenth on premises.

Established in 1989 with the incorporation of the former polytechnic, the Company of the University of East London Limited (trading as ELCO Ltd) is a closed company within the Companies Acts providing a legal framework for commercial income-generating activities in support of the University. With two full-time and two part-time administrative staff, the company also markets commercial opportunities arising within the University through membership of chambers of commerce, attendance at conferences and exhibitions, direct mail contact with companies, and personal presentations. Gross turnover for 1991-2 was £1.2 million.

The Company covenants pre-tax profit back to the University. In addition ELCO has purchased from the University goods and services (staff time, accommodation, catering, reprographics) approaching £1 million. Examples of some projects are a national programme for Ford Motor Company employees, a major research programme for the National Curriculum and various projects with the London East Training and Enterprise Council. All short course provision is through ELCO, including in-company training and 'open' courses for a wider audience.

MISSION

In 1992 the University established a strategic plan for the subsequent five years. This included the following mission statement and objectives:

The mission of the University of East London is to provide the highest possible quality of education, training, research and consultancy, in order to meet the needs of individuals of the communities and enterprises in our region.

The objectives of the University are under constant review to ensure their relevance and responsiveness to changing needs and demands. Those currently obtaining are:

- To improve academic quality in teaching and research.
- To aim to achieve a steady growth in student numbers to meet a target of a 50% increase by the end of the decade.
- To enhance amongst staff and students a pride in the institution coupled with a strong sense of community spirit.
- To widen access further for mature, non-traditionally qualified and ethnic minority students.
- To provide flexible and responsive study patterns and modes of learning.
- To develop an academic presence in London Docklands.
- Actively to encourage East Londoners to study at the University of East London.
- To develop as a centre of excellence for the study of East London, its culture, social, economic and political history.
- To work with our local communities on the basis of informed advice to improve the quality of life.
- To increase the international dimension of the student experience.
- To promote equal opportunities in line with the University's Equal Opportunities Policy Statement.

CHAPTER 2
To the East of London

The colleges which evolved into the University of East London were founded in areas which at one time constituted a number of adjoining rural parishes in the southwestern corner of the ancient county of Essex, bordered to the south by the river Thames, and to the west by the river Lea. At their nearest point they were less than four miles east of the City of London. However the capital's influence transformed this part of Essex during the later nineteenth and early twentieth centuries. The parishes increasingly had more in common with urban sprawl than with the rest of the county, but since they remained outside the London County Council they were often collectively referred to as metropolitan Essex.

The first to succumb was the parish of West Ham. In 1821 a population of less than 10,000 was concentrated around the three northern settlements of Stratford, West Ham and Plaistow. Milling had been a local industry since Domesday, while paper making, distilling and textiles also flourished around the five channels of the river Lea. Most of the parish was either laid down for agriculture, or consisted of estuarial marshland. By the turn of the twentieth century it had become the industrial heartland of the southeast of England (Marriott, 1988).

In 1839 the Eastern Counties Railway Company (later the Great Eastern) built a link from London to Norwich, thus ensuring that West Ham was no longer remote from the capital. The area's potential was soon recognised by entrepreneurial Victorian businessmen. Within a few years Stratford became the site of an extensive railway depot and locomotive works, boasting an engine a week, a carriage a day and a wagon an hour (Howarth & Wilson, 1907, p161), while the rail network had been extended through the south of the borough. The contractors that built the line took the opportunity to purchase a large expanse of open grazing land, virtually the whole of the southernmost part of the parish that adjoined the Thames. There, they constructed the Victoria Dock which opened in 1855. This was followed (particularly from the 1870s) by an extraordinary period of industrial development as heavy industry moved in to take advantage of the wharfage facilities on the Thames and the lower Lea. When the Albert Dock opened to shipping in 1880, the two and a half mile system of docks extended across the whole of the southern promontory through neighbouring East Ham, isolating Silvertown and part of North Woolwich. The King George V dock was completed in 1921. Nearby the giant Gas Light & Coke Company's works was the largest in the world when it opened on the banks of the Thames in 1870. Extending from East Ham into North Woolwich and Barking, it drew a large part of its workforce from Canning Town and generated a ready supply of coal by-products for subsidiary industries. West Ham became a major manufacturing area, where raw material could be landed and processed for the consumption of the largest consumer centre in the world, London.

The opportunities for employment attracted an attendant industrial workforce. Drawn to the area by the agricultural decline of East Anglia, and from London, the population expanded at a rapid rate. By 1901 more than

267,000 people lived in West Ham, and it was already the ninth most populous town in England. (Powell, 1973). The northern areas of West Ham were the most affluent, for they were more established residential areas and had more building space. Poorer parts of Stratford housed a considerable workforce for the railway depot, but it was also West Ham's administrative centre, containing the town hall, magistrates' court and other municipal buildings. Forest Gate, Plaistow and Upton were almost wholly residential.

The most deprived parts of West Ham were in the south, where the building of slum housing had followed industrial expansion. A speculative building boom that began in the 1870s, and over which the local authorities had little control, resulted in cheap, jerry built houses owned by absentee landlords. Much of the available work was unskilled and on casual terms. Poverty and hardship were rife.

It was such harsh industrial and social conditions as those which existed in West Ham, which spurred the gasworker's struggle for an eight hour day, the dock strike of 1889 and the early successes of a new political movement. In 1892 Keir Hardie 'the man in the cloth cap' (Taylor, 1977) was briefly elected to represent West Ham South, as the first independent Labour MP in the country. Similarly, in 1898 West Ham elected the first Labour dominated town council in British history.

In the parishes of Leyton and Walthamstow, by comparison, hardly any industry settled at all, but these areas were among the fastest growing during the 1880s and 1890s respectively. Migration from London was encouraged by the construction of railways: when the Great Eastern Railway built Liverpool Street station, it was bound by statute to run a cheap rate workman's train to Edmonton and Walthamstow each day, and the company expanded its services under the 1883 Cheap Trains Act.

Large scale speculative building of cheap terraced housing created a Victorian commuter belt. Unlike the sumptuous middle-class villas of Ealing, Surbiton or Sidcup, houses in Leyton and Walthamstow were built to conform to the basic standards of the 1875 Public Health Act, as many as forty to the acre laid out in gridiron street patterns, they were 'arid, unrelieved vistas of stock bricks and slates', (Jackson, 1973). Here were the homes of clerks, artisans and other respectable working people. Argyle described the poorest quarter of Walthamstow in 1889 as 'little Bethnal Green', comparing it to the old East End (Argyle, 1902).

In 1914, the expansion of built-up London into Essex stretched almost unbroken through West Ham and East Ham to the ancient town of Barking. Leyton and Walthamstow were booming, with a combined population of more than a quarter of a million. While other adjacent areas were rapidly developing suburbs – the combined populations of Ilford, Wanstead, Woodford and Chigwell rose from 31,766 in 1891 to 118,698 in 1911.

At the end of the war, Lloyd George promised the nation 'homes fit for heroes'. Legislation encouraged municipal housing schemes, by offering government subsidies. The London County Council's solution to its chronic housing problem was the construction of new estates at the fringes of the metropolis. The Becontree estate, 'the largest municipal housing estate in the world' (LCC, 1937) was laid out on a 3,000 acre site near the Essex village of Dagenham. Families uprooted from the relative squalor of inner London were given a fresh start in a purpose built township. By 1932 more than 100,000 people lived in LCC housing at Becontree (Young, 1939).

Industrial expansion continued eastwards of Barking, the Thames river bank proving attractive to heavy industry. Ten thousand men were employed in the construction of a coal-fired power station at Creekmouth, 'a desolate spot' (CLESC, 1925). The Ford Motor Company arrived at Dagenham from Manchester in 1931, and occupied a vast 600 acre site downstream from Dagenham Dock. Reclamation of marshland for the site required the local manufacture of some 22,000 piles, to carry the reinforced concrete rafts upon which the factory was constructed (DFBIBC, 1951). Other large companies located nearby manufactured vehicle bodies, wheels and variety of components for the automobile industry. May & Baker, the manufacturing chemists and inventors of the wonder drug 'M&B 693', migrated from their Battersea premises to the eastern fringe of the Becontree development in 1934.

Industrial settlement in Walthamstow and Leyton was dominated by light engineering, the manufacture of electrical goods, plastics, clothing and the furniture trades. Many businesses settling in these areas had migrated across the river Lea from the East End, or other parts of the county of London.

Meanwhile, West Ham, which advertised itself as 'London's Industrial Centre and Gateway to the World' in 1936, was already slipping into a slow economic decline. The shortage of land for development encouraged new industries to look elsewhere, while established companies struggled during the slump. In 1931 the highest unemployment levels in the southeast of England could be found in West Ham. Over a quarter of the insured labour force were registered unemployed, more than half of them signed on at the Canning Town labour exchange in the south of the borough (Marriott, 1989).

By the 1930s, the earliest metropolitanised districts of Essex, West Ham, East Ham, Leyton and Walthamstow, had already experienced their highest concentrations of population. In West Ham, population peaked at more than 318,000 in 1925 and had slowly begun to decline as people moved away, some seeking new jobs, others aspiring to more prosperous suburbs. It was a trend that was hastened by the advent of war with Germany in 1939.

As part of the capital's industrial base, West Ham was heavily bombed during the second world war. Overall, the borough suffered more than any other part of metropolitan Essex, its population virtually halved between 1938 and 1941. While casualties were much lighter than expected, many people were evacuated or left the area on their own initiative never to return. The population recovered to no more than 170,993 in 1951. Out of 51,000 residential properties roughly 14,000 (27 per cent) were destroyed and virtually every other home in the borough suffered some degree of damage (West Ham 1952). Typically, the poorest residential areas in the west and south of the borough had suffered most from bomb damage as a result of their proximity to industry and the docks. Neighbouring East Ham also suffered, but the scale of destruction to homes was quite unlike that in West Ham, since industrial targets (such as the docks) and housing were less intermingled. The more salubrious Essex suburbs escaped relatively lightly, although Ilford held the unenviable record of receiving more V2 rocket attacks within its boundaries than any other part of the Greater London area (Longmate, 1985).

Post-war planning for the reconstruction of the greater London area was driven by the policies of decentralisation of population and industry from central and suburban areas of the capital. Eight new towns ringed London in hitherto rural areas: Essex got Harlow and Basildon. The LCC meanwhile completed a number of its own housing schemes in Essex at Chingford Hatch, Debden, Hainault and Aveley. But Barking, Dagenham, Ilford, and Wanstead & Woodford were still growing in the 1950s.

In 1965 legislation pushed the administrative boundaries of London further out, so that it more or less matched the limits of the suburbs. The LCC was superseded by the Greater London Council (GLC). Adjacent local authorities found themselves merging. The county boroughs of East Ham and West Ham reluctantly became the London Borough of Newham. Leyton and Walthamstow became the London Borough of Waltham Forest. Barking and Dagenham were redesignated as the London Borough of Barking, until local civic pride forced the addition of Dagenham in 1981 (Hebbert, 1991).

Inner city renewal schemes of the 1960s were characterised by the construction of tower blocks, and many were built in Newham. In common with other local authorities, both East Ham and West Ham had begun to look to high-rise flats as the solution to their housing problems a decade earlier. The partial collapse of Ronan Point in Custom House in 1968, which killed 5 people, has been described as 'one of those chance occurrences which became symbolic of a whole sea-change in attitudes': it wasn't just mortal flesh or the credibility of construction methods which suffered when an old lady on the 18th floor lit her gas cooker. The explosion heralded a general loss of faith in the 'New Jerusalem' that Britain's architects and planners had built out of the rubble and squalor of the past (Stevenson, 1991). Nevertheless there were 111 council owned blocks over 5 storeys high within the borough in 1974. Some had as many as 22 floors. The Queens Road development was planned for 28 (Dunleavy, 1981).

London's industrial and economic vigour has always been a magnet for people looking for jobs, homes, and security, and the development of metropolitan Essex had drawn a flow of population out from the capital's inner core and attracted others from surrounding counties, or other parts of Britain. Occasionally migrating industries even brought their own workforce with them. Other nationalities also arrived, from the late nineteenth century, chiefly from Europe. Some displaced by war, others to escape persecution. Small communities from more far flung lands settled around the dock areas.

Since the 1950s Asians and Afro-Caribbeans began to settle in significant numbers in Newham, though generally it was not the first choice for immigrants in the early post-war period. Afro-Caribbeans had tended to settle elsewhere in London and many Asians first settled in the north of England and the west Midlands, where they worked in the factories and textile mills, before redundancy prompted moves southwards. Others had moved out of Tower Hamlets, where they had been employed as machinists or in the rag trade (NMP/CARF, 1991). Some have since moved outwards to neighbouring suburbs and to Essex, following a traditional migrants' path.

Newham can claim to be one of the most ethnically diverse boroughs in London and community relations have been continually dogged by outbreaks of racial friction. The Council made headlines in 1984, by becoming the first housing authority in the country to evict a white family for racial harassment. It still has one of the worst reputations for racially motivated crime.

By the late 1950s many Londoners might have agreed with Prime Minister Macmillan's assertion that they had never had it so good. It was the afterglow of Britain's wartime triumph. Many were enjoying a standard of living far above what they had previously known. Rationing had finally finished, more people were able to buy their first television set or car. The country had a national health service to be proud of. Jobs were plentiful, and for city commuters 'the new office world' was in the ascendancy: it was the hey-day of the typing pool (Humphries and Taylor, 1986).

With the war over Britain revitalised its old colonial and commonwealth links, and in 1956 the Port of London handled a record 70 million tons of cargo, transferred to an average of 1000 ships that docked each week (Humphries and Taylor,1986). But the disintegration of the Commonwealth, and the independence of colonies which followed was a blow to Britain's trade. Neither did the country compete with the industrial giants such as America or the re-constructed former axis powers, Japan and West Germany.

As a manufacturing centre London was in serious decline by the 1970s. Some companies closed completely and smaller firms were particularly at risk. Others had already moved out of London, encouraged by policies of decentralisation, site congestion, obsolescent premises and labour shortages. In the eight years between 1966-74 east and south east London boroughs bore the brunt of factory closures or relocations. Worst hit was Southwark on the south bank of the Thames, which lost 19,300 manufacturing jobs during this period. Newham lost at least 30 per cent of its manufacturing employment, accounting for some 12,100 jobs, and Barking & Dagenham a tenth of its manufacturing jobs (8,700) but Waltham Forest lost a quarter (5,800) (Dennis, 1978).

A study of industrial decline in Newham's Canning Town employment exchange area found that over the six year period 1966-72 there was a net job loss of 11,500. The sectors most affected were ship repair, chemicals and petroleum, general shipping and port activities. Six multinational companies, P & O, Unilever, Harland & Wolff, Tate & Lyle, Furness Withey and Vestey accounted for three quarters of all losses. Companies moving into the area had too few jobs to offer, since they were often interested only in bulk storage space. A postscript for the following five year period noted an additional 9,000 redundancies (CTCDP, 1977).

Ford meanwhile, began to redirect work to plants in other countries during the 1970s, leading to what one author has described as the 'disintegration' of its Dagenham works (Hamilton, 1991). Whereas the company had actually made the steel for such popular early cars as the Anglia and Cortina on site at Dagenham, assembly and component manufacture for later models was increasingly switched to the European continent. Thousands of jobs were shed throughout the 1970s and 1980s, mainly through voluntary redundancy. The works foundry closed in 1984, and research and development were located further out in Essex, at Brentwood. The giant Dagenham plant now chiefly assembles small cars and produces engine units.

Without the benefit of large scale re-investment the Port of London had gradually been losing trade to such modernised continental ports as Rotterdam and Hamburg. Greatly increasing reliance on trade with the European Economic Community (EEC) favoured coastal ports such as Felixstowe and Dover. Deteriorating industrial relations with the dockers were exacerbated by the Port of London Authority's decision to concentrate investment in Tilbury docks further downstream, and equip it for containerisation. The East India Docks in Tower Hamlets ceased operating in 1967, heralding more than a decade of closures and redundancies. By 1975 the Royal Docks in Newham were handling less than a third of the cargo they had handled five years earlier (LBN, 1976), and by 1981 they too had closed.

A Department of Environment study of urban deprivation in 1983 identified Newham as the second most deprived local authority area in the country, after neighbouring Hackney (DOE, 1983).

The closure of the Royal Docks prompted the government's creation of the London Docklands Development Corporation (LDDC), with the intention of a market-led strategy to regenerate the derelict dockland areas of Southwark, Tower Hamlets and Newham. In the first twelve years of operation £1,548 million of public money was spent and £5,944 million of private investment contractually committed. A further £3,200 million of private money has been committed in principle. There has been investment in infrastructure, the reclamation of 1,539 acres of derelict land, public utilities, road systems and the Docklands Light Railway. An airport in the Royal Docks now offers flights to 12 European cities. The LDDC claims the completion of 16,700 new homes, the doubling of total employment to 50,000, and the planting of over 100,000 trees planted (LDDC, 1993). But despite these impressive statistics there have been set-backs. Redevelopment of the Royal Docks was delayed in 1990 when developers pulled out of a plan to develop the biggest single site in Docklands. Olympia & York, developers of Britain's tallest building at Canary Wharf on the Isle of Dogs, went bankrupt in May 1992. The 1991 census indicates that the three dockland boroughs still have some of the highest rates of unemployment in London.

The redevelopment of the Docklands, impressive and controversial though it is has been, is not the whole story. There are other major planning proposals which would radically affect the former rural parishes in this corner of Essex.

Barking & Dagenham council in accord with National Power are proposing to develop 800 acres of 'prime riverfront land' at Barking Reach. The scheme envisages 6,000 new homes, parkland and the improvement of conservation habitats. Industrial development will include a new gas-fired power station (LB&D, undated). It is hoped that the scheme will provide enough jobs to reduce unemployment of 12.7 per cent of men and 5.4 per cent of women in 1991 (excluding those on government schemes), among the highest rates in outer London boroughs. However, Fords, the borough's largest employer announced hundreds of further job losses at Dagenham in 1992 and cut car production (Guardian, 1992a,1992b).

Some £37 million of public money has been allocated to the successful Stratford City Challenge bid. Newham

Council, in partnership with commercial interests and the
local community, have produced a plan which aims to
attract £280 million from other sources and revitalise
the Stratford area. A range of projects, including the
creation of a technology centre for a local school and
major improvements to the shopping centre and station,
are under way (SDP, 1992).

All of these ventures are now seen as integral to the
successful exploitation of the East Thames Corridor: an
area containing more than 1.6 million people, which
extends eastwards on either side of the river; from Stratford
through Tilbury in Essex, and from Greenwich to the Isle
of Sheppey in Kent. This is meant to become the United
Kingdom's gateway to Europe, and equally, the entry point
for Europe into London and the United Kingdom. As a
DOE report eloquently puts it

> The strategy for the western end of the corridor can
> exploit the potential synergy between the East London
> International Passenger Station, London City Airport,
> the transport node of Stratford, the uniquely attractive
> Royal Docks and the eastwards-expanding City, punc-
> tuated by Canary Wharf.
>
> The strategy could entice European visitors to treat
> East London as a destination rather than a transit
> camp. The IPS and the Airport provide the means
> by which the European visitor arrives in East London,
> the City and Docklands provide the motive, and the
> opportunity is provided by the waterside sites of the
> Royals, developed as a destination of world city status.
> (DOE, 1993)

CHAPTER 3
Civic Enterprise

The origins of the University of East London lie in two bursts of civic energy in metropolitan Essex. Each was a response to the development described in the last chapter. The first was in West Ham, spurred by the creation of the county borough in 1889 and the provisions of the Technical Instruction Act of the same year. The second was in the 1930s, when the county of Essex responded to the movement of population out of London into new housing estates.

The most obvious characteristic of modern London (indeed metropolitan cities in general), is that a great many people live in and around it. The advent of railways, and then the automobile, have cut travel times so drastically that Greater London stretches over a dozen miles east of Aldgate to Romford and beyond. Some London commuters may not live in the suburbs at all, travelling from any number of destinations in the home counties, like Brighton, Colchester or Huntingdon, each working day. Decentralisation of population and housing and similar distribution of economic activity and jobs has even led some geographers to think in terms of London as a 'megalopolis' extending 75 miles from the centre and stretching from Dorset to Suffolk (Warnes, 1991).

Such large concentrations are familiar enough to contemporary Britain. It was the generations of Victorians who experienced the full impact of the world's first industrial economy and society in full flood, witnessing the mass suburbanisation of London – 'the world city', as Asa Briggs described it (Briggs, 1968). Within the central area, whose boundaries later more or less adopted by London County Council, the capital's population grew from a mere 959,310 in 1801 to 2,363,341 in 1851 and by the end of the century stood had almost doubled again to 4,536,267, while the metropolitanised areas of counties beyond experienced an increase of more than six fold, from 317,594 in 1851 to 2,045,135 in 1901. Between 1881 and 1891 the four communities with the highest rate of population growth in England included West Ham and Leyton (the others were Tottenham and Willesden). Between 1891 and 1901 the fastest growing four included East Ham and Walthamstow, with Croydon and Hornsey. What this felt like at the time can be imagined from H G Wells's bleak description in 1909 of 'the unorganised, abundant substance of some tumorous growth-process, a process which indeed bursts all the outlines of the affected carcase and protrudes such masses as ignoble, comfortable Croydon or tragic, impoverished West Ham' (Wells, 1953). Urban growth on this scale at last prompted the creation of effective local administration.

The last three decades of the nineteenth century were a great period for the invention of local public institutions, and many of the administrative patterns then established survived until today. It was the Local Government Act of 1888 that set up county councils, based on the historic shires (including Essex), to take over the administrative functions (mainly highways and bridges) of the quarter sessions, thus replacing the aristocratic by the democratic principle in local government (the latter principle is now under threat from the establishment of 'agencies'). Larger boroughs, normally those with over 50,000 people, could become county boroughs, exercising the same powers and duties as counties.

West Ham benefited immediately from the Act. Before 1886 it had been merely an Essex parish, with powers and revenues quite inadequate to deal with human, urban and industrial squalor. Since 1856 a Local Board of Health, created in response to inadequate sewerage and sanitation, had powers to improve sanitation, manage the supply of water and regulate offensive trades in the parish. It re-organised the West Ham fire brigade, took over the maintenance of highways and building control and appointed a medical officer of health. It became the most influential body in the parish:

> the Local Board was authorised to introduce bylaws, subject to the approval of the General Board (of Health), and to seek additional powers by enacting legislation through Parliament...the Board was able to gain the authority to increase the number of its members, construct a town hall and offices, purchase land compulsorily and raise finance to undertake ambitious works of construction and improvement. (Marriott, 1984, p92)

Even so,

> The Board could rarely act with complete autonomy since it had to contend with the presence in different spheres of local administration with the vestry, the Havering and Dagenham Commissioners, the Board of Guardians, the Thames and Lee Conservancies, and the Essex Quarter Sessions, which frequently had competing interests. (Marriott, 1984, p93)

Its own administration was often defective and there were several cases of fraud and vote rigging (Powell, 1973). 'Pressure from the increasing number of poor living in squalid and overcrowded conditions for better facilities was successfully resisted by the larger ratepayers.' Rates were generally kept lower than those in neighbouring metropolitan and suburban districts, and in the last ten years of the Board's existence rates were reduced from 4s. 2d to 2s. 0d: 'The consequence was a totally inadequate revenue with which to function effectively. Its record of public work was poor; sanitation, poverty, housing, communication and facilities were all neglected, provoking constant criticism in the local press' (Marriott, 1984, p93).

From 1870 the Board considered incorporation as a borough, largely to avoid absorption by the Metropolitan Board of Works, with higher rates and stricter by-laws. A first petition in 1879 failed: the case put forward was 'ill-considered and weak' (Marriott, 1984, p96).

Renewed efforts in 1885 were more organised: a petition in favour of incorporation which included the majority of the largest manufacturers in the parish collected 18,000 signatures. The opponents of incorporation numbered only 57, and many of these were connected with the liquor trade and would have welcomed the less restrictive metropolitan licensing laws (Marriott, 1984, p96). The rest simply feared the Board of Works:

> The very worst thing that could happen would be to fall into the hands of this bloated and overswollen authority, bending under the burden of gigantic debt. The best thing for West Ham is that it should acquire the completest power of self-government to aid and foster its energies and its developments. (SE, 1885a)

> It is impossible to exaggerate the effect of local self government in moulding the destinies of England, in developing her strength, and making her at the same time the chief among nations and the one example of combined freedom and order...local government

was our one, and sufficient, buckler against assaults of despotic power. But for it England would have sunk under a tyranny worse than that of Russia; with it, she has conquered her oppressors and forced them to become Englishmen. (SE, 1885b)

As Marriott said, 'The two pillars (of the argument) were the preservation of liberty and the prevention of rate increases; and yet the evidence marshalled in these was at best conjectural' (Marriott, 1984, p97).

When West Ham became a municipal borough in July 1886 the council acquired all the powers formerly held by the local board, including those granted by Parliamentary legislation in a series of extension of powers acts throughout the Board's thirty year existence. West Ham was actually endowed with higher powers than those held by most other corporations (Marriott, 1984, p99). It received county borough status in 1889 under the terms of the 1888 Local Government Act. This gave it independence from Essex County Council with complete control of all local services except the poor law and education.

It was not long before the new county and county borough councils were given new powers: among the first of these was for technical education. Since 1870 local school boards had been given the task, with the power to raise a rate, of filling the gaps left by the churches and other voluntary agencies, in elementary education. As W E Forster said, when introducing the successful Elementary Education Bill to the House of Commons in February 1870:

Upon this speedy provision of elementary education depends also our national powers...and if we are to hold our position among men of our own race or among the nations of the world, we must make up the smallness of our numbers by increasing the intellectual force of the individual. (Hansard, 1870)

The hopes of the period were summed up by Sir Arthur
Conan Doyle in *The Naval Treaty*:

> Holmes was sunk in profound thought, and hardly
> opened his mouth until we had passed Clapham Junc-
> tion.
>
> "It's a very cheering thing to come to London by any
> of these lines which run high and allow you to look
> down upon the houses like this."
>
> I thought he was joking, for the view was sordid
> enough, but he soon explained himself.
>
> "Look at those big, isolated clumps of buildings
> rising up above the slates, like brick islands in a lead
> coloured sea."
>
> "The Board schools."
>
> "Lighthouses my boy! Beacons of the future! Cap-
> sules, with hundreds of bright little seeds in each, out
> of which will spring the wiser, better England of the
> future...." (Conan Doyle, 1974, p225)

The school boards remained responsible for elementary
education until they were abolished in 1902 and their
powers and duties transferred to the counties and county
boroughs. Elementary education was made compulsory in
1880. At the same time private effort had been directed
into technical education. In particular the Polytechnic
had been founded in Regent Street by Quintin Hogg,
and Finsbury Technical College by the City and Guilds
of London Institute (see Burgess and Pratt, 1970). Such
institutions as polytechnics were intended, according to the
Charity Commissioners, to

> promote the industrial skill, general knowledge, and
> well-being of young men and women belonging to the
> poorer classes. (Royal Commission, 1913)

Government action came with the Technical Instruction Act 1889. This provided that

> a local authority may from time to time out of the local rate supply or aid the supply of technical or manual instruction, to such extent and on such terms as the authority think expedient.... (Acts, 1889)

It explained that

> The expression "technical instruction" shall mean instruction in the principles of science and art applicable to industries, and in the application of special branches of science and art specific industries or employments. It shall not include teaching the practice of any trade or industry or employment, but, save as aforesaid, shall include instruction in the branches of science and art with respect to which grants are for the time being made by the Department of Science and Art, and any other form of instruction (including modern languages and commercial and agricultural subjects), which may for the time being be sanctioned by that Department by a minute laid before Parliament and made on the representation of local authority that such a form of instruction is required by the circumstances of the district.

Similarly,

> The expression 'manual instruction' shall mean instruction in the use of tools, processes of agriculture, and modelling in clay, wood, or other material. (Acts, 1889)

The Act was adoptive in that it came into effect in an area only if actually adopted by a local authority. It permitted county, borough and urban sanitary authorities to supply or support technical instruction to the extent of the product of a 1d. rate. These authorities could also appoint a committee wholly or partly chosen from their own members to carry out their functions under the Act, except for the power of raising a rate or borrowing money.

In the next year the Chancellor of the Exchequer, Viscount Goschen, was able, by passing on to them a windfall popularly called 'whisky money', to provide the wherewithal for 'a most important educational progress' (Ensor, 1936, p204).

The whisky money was an oddity. The Local Government Act, 1888, as originally introduced, had proposed to transfer liquor licensing from the justices to the county councils, arming the latter with compulsory powers to close redundant public houses and a special revenue to compensate the licence-holders. Unfortunately the liquor trade disliked compulsion and the temperance party denounced compensation, so the clauses were dropped. But Goschen had reduction of licences very much at heart, and the growth of drunkenness during the prosperity years 1887-90 impelled him to try again. In his Budget of 1890 he put an extra 6d. on a gallon of spirits, and with this and a third of the beer duty formed a new fund for compensating licence-holders. Again the same union of opposites defeated the plan, but the money had already been voted, and he persuaded parliament to pass it on to the county councils through the Local Taxation (Customs and Excise) Act, 1890. An amendment by Arthur Ackland MP specifically empowered the authorities to spend the money on technical instruction over and above what was spent from the rates.

By the turn of the century the amount of whisky money thus spent on technical education was nearly £900,000, or nearly 90 per cent of all public expenditure for this purpose. Between 1890 and 1902 the whisky money had built twelve polytechnics or technical institutions in

London, thirteen in the rest of the country and more than 100 science schools (Ministry of Education, 1950). One of these institutions was a new technical institute in West Ham.

THE FORERUNNERS IN WEST HAM

There were already many organisations with an interest in technical education in West Ham in 1889, before the proposal for a technical institute was even mooted.

The creation of counties and county boroughs had not affected the school boards set up after the Education Act 1870, and elementary education remained the responsibility of the boards and of voluntary bodies. The latter had provided schools locally at least since 1723 when the first recorded charity school was opened in association with the parish church. (Simms, p145). West Ham's school board, established in 1871, was reputed to be one of the first in England. The membership of the board, elected separately from the borough council, was dominated by a Progressive majority until 1895, and then by Conservatives until it was superseded under the 1902 Education Act (Simms, 1973, p144). Occasionally a councillor might also be elected to the board, as was T.P. Whitty, a carpenter who put the board's view to the council.

During the 32 years of the board's existence the school population of West Ham rose to around 60,000. In 1902 Board Schools had the capacity for 53,533 pupils, non-board schools for 8,646 pupils. (WHSB, 1902). By 1903 the board had built 43 elementary schools, a school for the deaf, one for physical and mental defectives, one for truants and two pupil teacher centres (Simms, 1973, p144).

An Education Department Inspector for the West Ham district reported in 1895:

The general features of the district of West Ham remain as before, the population increases at the same rapid rate, and the tendency of the number of children to outgrow the supply of school accommodation is as striking as ever. Since my last report, two years ago, 18 new board schools have been opened. Eight of these are temporary, but arrangements have already been made for the erection of permanent schools to take their place....The whole of the district is under school boards, and all of these are doing their duty well in the face of difficulties. The district is not a wealthy one, the bulk of the inhabitants are of the labouring class, and the ratio of children to adults is higher than in any other part of England.... (Sharpe, 1896, p4)

The school board was alert to the allocations of funds for technical instruction. As early as June 1888 the clerk had 'laid on the table a copy of the Bill on Technical Education' (WHSB, 1888). As the educational body within the borough the board obviously expected to benefit from any funds raised by the council, and appointed a sub-committee to co-ordinate in the process (WHSB, 1889a, b, 1890). But applications for funds were unsuccessful, and a consultation with the council and the Carpenters' Company (see below) had no apparent effect (SE, 1891a).

The Carpenters' Company, an ancient guild founded in 1333, owned a large tract of marshland at Stratford on which they had built an estate. The company instructed its clerk, on March 3rd, 1885 to write to the West Ham school board:

The Court of the Carpenters' Company, feeling an interest in the industrial training of the children of the Artisan Classes, especially on their own estates, would be glad to learn if the West Ham School Board can suggest any way in which the Company can aid in carrying out this object. (Old Carpentarians, 1964)

At the beginning of 1886 the company had decided

to spend up to £2,000 a year on objects connected with its craft, including technical education, lectures, and exhibitions. A further £500 was to be spent on general education, scholarships to universities and gifts to libraries and schools.

A sub-committee considered what scheme could be adopted for the benefit of tenants on the Stratford estate. They met with the Minister of the Baptist chapel in Carpenters' Road, the Reverend G. Towner, at Stratford on February 11th 1886. Subsequently a plot of land was bought in Jupp Road (behind the present Duncan House). Within the year it was opened as an evening institute with a reading room and classes in carpentry, joinery, plumbing, geometry, cookery and mechanical drawing. Provision was made for a gymnasium, and a covered swimming pool was also added. Later, in 1891, the premises of the evening institute were also used as a secondary day school, and Mr Towner became headmaster.

But the fortunes of the Carpenters' school and technical institute were affected by the opening of the West Ham Technical Institute and, by the development of municipal secondary schooling. Eventually the Company offered to hand the school over to the borough council, but the offer was not accepted. The school and the evening institute were closed in July 1905 (West Ham, 1905, p1677), and the gymnasium and baths were transferred to municipal control for the use of the public (West Ham, 1905, p2221).

Another initiative was that of Thames Iron Works. During the late nineteenth century this firm was one of England's leading shipbuilders, providing commercial and naval vessels for a dozen countries. It was a major employer in West Ham and an early provider of technical education within the borough until it closed in 1912.

From 1880 the company was run by Arnold Hills, a paternalistic employer who encouraged the organization of social activities attached to the iron works. There were cricket, cycling, athletics, boating and football clubs. Choral and drama societies were also established, and Hills took an active part in the affairs of the iron works temperance club. He was also a fervent vegetarian.

The company first established 'science classes' in 1887, with a series of lectures on applied mechanics, which were endorsed by the Science and Art Department. Forty members of staff attended, and encouraged by the initial success, other courses of lectures were given in magnetism, electricity, and mathematics. By 1895 all classes were still compatible with the Science and Art Department's syllabus, but with the emphasis on practical application to current work at the yard. Those in 'practical plane and solid geometry' for example, were advised for 'all pattern makers, fitters, platers, in fact everyone who wants to understand how to read a drawing...' (TIWG, 1895a, p115). Students of the highly specialized naval architecture classes had the opportunity of winning various prizes, awarded by the Thames Iron Works, the Shipwrights' Company, and the City and Guilds of London Institute. The explicit principle behind all the classes was,

> The uneducated worker may do well enough work that he has done before, but when new jobs have to be undertaken, and new processes commenced, it is the man who has educated himself who has the advantage. (TIWG, 1895b, p19)

Although figures are unavailable, it appears that numbers attending the company's classes were not always consistent. In 1891 a diminished attendance in all classes was being blamed on fresh competition from other institutions, engendered by the effects of the Technical Instruction Act. And despite a reorganization of content, most were cancelled in 1893-4, for which a slump in business was blamed. In 1898 all 'science classes' at the iron works were discontinued, and employees encouraged to attend the new technical institute, which also assumed responsibility for the specialised teaching of naval architecture.

The major supplier of technical instruction in West Ham before the advent of the municipal technical institute, was the Eastern Counties (later the Great Eastern) Railway Mechanics Institute, established as early as 1851, and originally housed within the precincts of the old Stratford railway station (long since demolished) near Angel Lane Bridge (Smith, D., p112). The Stratford works was a vast depot for locomotive and rolling stock construction and maintenance, which supplied the entire rail network. It was the borough's major regular employer of labour, with a workforce at Stratford of 1,500 in 1850, and 4,970 in 1895 (Howarth and Wilson, 1907, p161).

The Mechanics Institute had a particular interest in the expenditure of West Ham's 'whisky money': it sought to benefit from a technical instruction grant in 1891, at a crucial time when the council were deciding how it should be spent. Only three months before, in March 1891 the institute had been inspected by a representative of the Science and Art Department. Contents of a memorandum sent to the school secretary were highly critical of facilities, particularly accommodation:

> The Science and Art work at this school still requires much encouragement and organization. Connected as it is with the most important Mechanics Institute in the Metropolitan district, with a membership roll of nearly 1,000 names, and situated in the midst of a dense artisan population, the school ought to be more prosperous in numbers and better equipped for Science teaching. None of the classrooms have any special fittings for experimental teaching, and most of them are small, and badly ventilated. No instruction in Practical Chemistry

or Practical Physics can be obtained nearer than the People's Palace. The remuneration of the teachers still depends in nearly all cases directly on the grant and fees, a system which acts as a discouragement on both the preliminary work absolutely necessary in certain sub-jects, and on the advanced work, in which the number of students is at present small. Students also often take up too many subjects, partly from want of guidance, partly from absence of regulations by the Committee, with the result that they get wearied before the session is over, and then stay away.... The provision of better accommodation for the educational work of this impor-tant centre, and the fuller recognition by the Committee of the desirability of continuous instruction in certain subjects, apart from their financial success, would, I am convinced enormously increase the efficiency of these classes, and enlarge the number of students attending them. (Science and Art Department 1891a)

The governing committee of the institute having venti-lated the criticism in the presence of James Holden, the Railway's chief engineer, noted that 'to fully remove the complaint would necessitate another building upon a more suitable site' (GER, 1891, p182).

One of the proposers of this resolution was trade unionist W.R. Athey, who had been a member of the institute's governing committee since 1886 (GER, 1886), a member of West Ham Council since 1889, and a member of the committee responsible for the expenditure of the borough's 'whisky money' – the Technical Instruction Act Committee. Athey drafted a letter from the Mechanics Institute to the Technical Instruction Act Committee, requesting a grant (GER, 1891, p191):

Having for many years provided Technical Instruction with valuable results for Wood and Iron Workers and students in other subjects, and being extremely anxious in the interest of working men who are housed in large numbers near our Institute, that there should be no cessation in this good and necessary work, our past educational record being the oldest and the largest providers of Science and Technological training in the Borough of West Ham, our school being then open to all applicants, justifies as we feel in asking for your best consideration in dispensing the grant obtained from Government in aid of Technical training. A very strong reason which should prevail and favour our application being, that the Guildhall Technical Committee have intimated that owing to the Corporation being supplied with money for this purpose they will cease their helpful monetary assistance at the end of the year. This will seriously hamper us and imperil the continuation of solid instruction in this district and we feel sure our application will receive at your hands the attention it deserves.

On the day that the Mechanics Institute Committee agreed to sending this request for a grant, the institute itself was being discussed by the Technical Instruction Act Committee. But any decisions were deferred, for the committee had decided that the fund at their disposal would not be spent entirely on education. Instead, they proposed to purchase land for a recreation ground in the south of the borough.

The London Society for the Extension of University Teaching periodically held evening lectures in West Ham from as early as 1879 (Soar, 1966, p98). By 1891 they had become so successful that the Stratford 'centre' at the Town Hall was second in examination performance of the London centres (SE, 1891b), and courses were also held at Canning Town. The success of these lectures convinced the local authority to set aside a little of the interest earned by the 'whisky money' to provide them at no cost to the public.

Councillor Horncastle remarked at the decisive council meeting in November 1891:

> At the lectures at Canning Town last year he saw men with grimy hands come in and take notes and he thought they ought to be encouraged. It would only be fair if a small portion of this fund should be devoted to technical lectures which would prepare the way for the great institution they were going to have later on. (SE, 1891b)

The following year saw the beginning of a series of free lectures, financed by the council and managed by the University Extension Society. At the first night in Stratford Professor Vivian Lewis spoke about 'the Chemistry of everyday life', to an audience of 700. An estimated 300 stayed behind afterwards to ask questions. In Canning Town the lectures were held at the Mansfield University Settlement (West Ham, 1892, p280). A third centre was added in 1893 at the request of the Forest Gate Ratepayers Association (West Ham, 1893, p356). But once the technical institute opened those courses at the Town Hall and Forest Gate were transferred to it.

These institutions were by no means the only ones providing technical instruction. Others included the Primrose Literary Institute, in Silvertown, connected with the Royal Primrose Soap Works; the Tate Institute, founded in Silvertown by the sugar manufacturers; the Church Institute; the School of Science and Art; the Conference Hall and Young Men's Christian Association; and three board schools – Maryland Point, Salway Place and Custom House (Science and Art Department, 1891b, p67).

The position of the board schools was anomalous, not to say illegal. The Education Act 1870 had given the school boards powers for elementary education only, yet the Government had encouraged them into Secondary and Technical in three ways. First, the Education Department offered grants not only for the 'obligatory' and 'class' subjects of the elementary schools, but for 'specific' subjects in the upper standards of these schools, including mathematics, science, agriculture, languages and commercial and domestic arts. Second, the Science and Art Department gave grants on the results of its own examinations. This encouraged the establishment of 'higher grade' board schools and 'higher tops' in board schools for pupils who had passed standard VII and were now doing more advanced work. Third, the Science and Art Department gave grants for 'organized science schools' – grouped science classes held in the daytime or in the evening in elementary, higher grade in other schools (Barnard, 1947, p234-5). This officially encouraged illegality was eventually challenged by the Cockerton judgement of 1901, leading to the reorganization of secondary education under the Education Act 1902 (Barnard, 1947, p244).

After the Technical Instruction Act 1889, West Ham borough council created a Technical Instruction Act Committee, to decide how any income might be used and in April 1890 had agreed to confer with an expectant West Ham School Board. (West Ham, 1890, p93). However, the Local Taxation Act 1890, had provided the council with an initial windfall of £4,600, and the committee recommended in June 1891, that the money be used to create a public recreation ground, in the south of the borough at Canning Town. (West Ham, 1891, p256).

This proposal elicited the support of the finance committee when they met two days later, probably because it offered the prospect of relief to the general rate. Less than twenty years earlier the West Ham local board's attempts to purchase Ham Park in the north of the parish, had twice been blocked by the opposition of a ratepayers' association unwilling to bear the extra financial burden. Now however, the capital for the purchase of land in the south was to be raised by means of a £20,000 loan from the Local Government Board, which would be repaid by interest accumulated on the investment of 'whisky money' (West Ham, 1891, p251). At least one member of the Technical Instruction Act Committee had in fact been agitating for a public park in Canning Town since 1885, which may partially explain the Committee's preference:

> Councillor White is an ardent advocate of Technical Education but considered the provision of a Recreation Ground so dire a necessity, and that it would confer so unspeakable a boon on the thickly populated district of the south, especially on the poor people, that he was prepared to sacrifice technical education for it, if there had been no alternative. (SEEG, 1891a)

Richard White was described by the local press as an 'uncompromising radical' and was said to favour the notion of an Independent Labour Party. He was in fact one of the local trade unionists elected to the council in 1886. As a representative of South West Ham, he had also campaigned for the provision of other public amenities in that part of the borough: a bridge over the Lea at Canning Town, a public hall, public baths and wash houses.

Another line of argument was pursued by a letter that appeared in the *Stratford Express*, identified only by the initials E W in which it was mentioned that the 'City Guilds' had intimated to the Carpenters' Company that as the council now possessed funds for technical education, then they would reduce their fund accordingly. Indeed the GER Mechanics Institute had referred to similar fears in their grant application to the council, using it as a means of bolstering their claim. Here, however, the argument was turned against them:

Thus, if the rich City Companies…are simply going to withdraw so much of their own money from West Ham as is equal to what they can get from our Corporation, it is plain that the technical instruction grant is not likely to do us much good. In these circumstances the choice is not so much between a park and technical education, as between a park or nothing at all. Then I do not blame the technical committee for going for the park. (SE, 1891c)

At the beginning of 1891 Mayor Henry Worland, a coal merchant, had spoken at a university extension prize giving ceremony in Stratford:

The study of chemistry and science was a branch of technical education, and though it would be necessary that a technical day school should be established in the borough, that all children on passing a certain examination might have the opportunity to acquire certain knowledge on technical subjects, still there ought to be means whereby adults could obtain that knowledge which they had not acquired in their earlier life. (SE, 1891d, p2)

The Mayor was referring to the prospect of the council's partial funding of new courses. He certainly appeared sympathetic to the principle of developing technical instruction. Yet when the Mechanics Institute committee called a public meeting outside the GER Works on July 18th, with the purpose of appointing a deputation to the council in protest at the way in which the 'whisky money' was to be spent, the Mayor was accused of voting in favour of the relief of rates. He had been a voting member of both the Finance and Technical Instruction Act Committees (SE, 1891e, p7).

The discussion on technical education dominated a five

and a half hour meeting of the full council on 14th July 1891. Councillor Whitty introduced a deputation from the School Board, represented by its chairman, who urged that the funds be spent on technical education, while Councillor Athey introduced similar deputations from the Great Eastern Railway's works, and the committee of the Mechanics Institute, represented by chief engineer James Holden.

Two local clergymen spoke in favour of a recreation ground. They were said to represent a variety of interested parties in the south of the borough, some 80,000 people, which included the Silvertown Ratepayers' Association, a number of cricket clubs and members of the various local unions:

> They asked for this park for many reasons; the aged people who had no resort but the street...the working men too, would not so often resort to the public house if they had some place of recreation provided for them. Then he pleaded for the young men who would soon have nowhere to play cricket, and for the children who could only play in the streets where they were in constant peril. (SEEG, 1891b, p5)

The council finally agreed to a plan which would raise capital for the provision of a recreation ground and public hall in the south of the borough, yet leave the £4,600 that had been intended for technical instruction untouched. A *Stratford Express* editorial suspected that the disputed scheme had finally been 'blown into space' because the Mayor had begun to doubt whether the Local Government Board would actually approve it (SE, 1891e).

A TECHNICAL INSTITUTE

Two days later, the Technical Instruction Act Committee were ready to propose that the 'whisky money' should be used to establish a technical institute, which would be administered by the council. It is not clear when the idea for such an institution was first conceived for West Ham; there is little evidence that it had ever been discussed before this meeting. Yet motions were tabled by the two councillors with respective interests in the Mechanics Institute, and the School Board, Mr. Athey and Mr. Whitty (West Ham, 1891, p296). Just what their respective motives were is unclear. They may have proposed the construction of a technical institute, to benefit the interests they represented. The Mechanics' Institute, for example was at that time specifically concerned about acquiring a new building. In the event the committee's proposal was accepted in principle by the council on 1st August 1891.

The School Board, and the Mansfield University Settlement at Canning Town, which had sought to benefit directly from the fund, were to be disappointed (West Ham, 1891, p377). The Great Eastern Railway Mechanics Institute later received a modest annual grant, but this was discontinued shortly after the Technical Institute opened (West Ham, 1892, p417). It was West Ham corporation that was to become the major provider of technical education within the borough.

In the early days technical instruction was closely linked in the minds of councillors with the provision of libraries. Indeed the early sub-committee of 16 members of the Technical Instruction Act and Library sub-committees combined in November 1891, to continue their function as the Public Libraries and Technical Instruction Committee, until superseded under the 1902 Education Act (West Ham, 1892, p26). Public attitudes to the adoption of the Public Libraries Act had first been tested in a poll in April 1887: 800 were for it, and 1,220 against. A second poll in November 1890 recorded 9,953 in favour and 3,538 against. A few months later a libraries committee was appointed and a rate was raised. Rokeby House was

opened in Stratford to supply the north of the borough and
a purpose built library was later opened in Canning Town,
in September 1893. The decision to house both library and
technical institute in the same building was apparently first
suggested in March 1892, and Parliamentary assent was
given in 1893 for the library to be paid for from technical
funds (SE, 1896, p5).

The technical institute took some seven years from
inception to completion. In 1892 the Technical Instruction Committee held a 'conversazione' at the Town Hall,
with the object of arousing interest in technical instruction.
Music was provided by a 'glee union' and the evening was
hosted and arranged by the incumbent Mayor, Alderman
Hay, who declared that 'The only unfortunate thing about
the tax was that the more drink there was consumed the
more money they would get for technical instruction'
(SE, 1892, p7). This may have been a little ironic since
he was described in 1890 as a 'refreshment contractor'
(Kelly's, 1890).

After a number of designs had been put forward by the
borough engineer's department, and presumably found
unsatisfactory, the proposed building became the subject
of a competition in 1893. Seventy-five entries were
submitted. The winning architects were Messrs Gibson
and Russell of Grays Inn Square (SE, 1896, p5).

The foundation stone was 'well and truly laid' on
October 29 1896 by the Mayor, Alderman William Crow
JP. In a long speech he referred to the origins of the
public library, and also to the working classes bettering
themselves:

The population of West Ham was largely – if not
entirely – of the industrial class, and it appeared in the
present day that the ordinary elementary education was
insufficient to enable people to make their way in the
world. They knew that unskilled labour was one of the

chief causes of bringing down the wages of the workers, and therefore any means that could be devised to raise wages legitimately and put the workers in a position to better themselves, must meet with approval generally. (SE, 1896, p5)

The opening ceremony of the library and technical institute took place on a 'brilliant' afternoon in October 1898. The building was decorated with gaily coloured bunting, and the band of the 1st Essex Artillery Volunteers played a selection of music. Crowds gathered in the street to watch the spectacle.

Just before the ceremony a commemorative bust was discreetly placed in the Water Lane entrance of the Institute. It was a tribute to Charles Mare whose local shipbuilding company had later become the prestigious Thames Iron Works.

Then the military formed a guard of honour at the main entrance, the great hall filled with guests, and civic dignitaries waited for the symbolic unlocking of the doors with a 'golden key' (FGWN, 1898, p7). The guest of honour, Mr John Passmore Edwards, a philanthropic publishing magnate, voiced the sense of local importance in affairs of Empire:

West Ham was trying to keep up with other countries; and if other large towns in Great Britain had imitated their example Germany would not be so far ahead. But it was not Germany he feared. There was another and still more rapidly expanding nation – America. That country was putting forth prodigious energy on sea and on land.... Looking all around he saw that unless we turned to the best account the advantages and opportunities we had we should be left behind in the race of the nations....

... We were the best destroyers in the world; we could

knock down a city like Alexandria to smithereens in an hour or two. Our instruments of destruction surpassed those of any other nation. What we wanted now were instruments of production equal to those of destruction, and then no German could beat us (Hear, hear). If we spent a quarter of the money in education we were now spending on the outlying defences of the country we should never be beaten. There was an interior defence – the education of the citizens; if they were not educated our industries would not be maintained, and our commerce would not flourish, and if our commerce did not keep up our industries could not prosper. (SE, 1898, p5)

The sense of satisfaction in civic enterprise was almost palpable. Within a year, however, much of the building had burned down.

On the 23rd October 1899 at about twenty past two in the morning, a fire was discovered in the advanced chemical laboratory. The alarm was raised, and the fire brigade called out. Meanwhile the caretaker fought the blaze with the rudimentary 'appliances' with which the building was equipped, but it was a futile effort. Despite the attendance of the council's three 'steamers', nine from London, and one from East Ham, the roof of the building and a considerable portion of the Institute was destroyed (West Ham, 1899, p1413).

Although the Stratford engine was promptly on the spot, and all the hydrants in the building were in use, it was impossible to check the spread of the flames. The help telegraphed for from the London Brigade was also nearly two hours in arriving, as owing to the dense fog the horses had to be walked the whole way. (SE, 1900, p5)

It took almost another year for the institute to be re-opened. It was re-built with improvements to the engineering and engine dynamo laboratories, while a smithy and foundry were also added. The chemistry department was located in a new block, separate from the main building, although the cause of the fire remained a mystery. In the meantime most classes were quickly relocated either at the School Board's premises in Water Lane, or at a council-owned house in the Romford Road, bought to provide the site of a public baths built later. Workshop classes remained in the college.

The re-opening of the Institute on October 18th 1900 coincided with that of the museum built next door. This building, later named after its chief benefactor Passmore Edwards, housed a large natural history collection belonging to the Essex Field Club. The club had originally proposed to establish a museum at Chelmsford several years before, but without success. Most of the leading Council members attended, including Alderman Athey who had been convicted under the Corrupt Practices Act that very week (SE, 1900b, p2).

Lady Warwick (who described herself as a member of the field club) opened the museum:

> She feared that the spirit of modern science had not sunk into the public mind and permeated the rank and file to that extent which was required by the age in which they lived. Their purses were ever open in the name of charity, philanthropy, missionary work, political organisation, and public sport, but science, upon which our welfare and our position in the scale of nations ultimately depended, had to go begging for its tens while thousands are forthcoming for other objects.

Mr Passmore Edwards, performing a function he had carried out two years earlier, declared the technical institute to be 'the people's university' (SE, 1900b, p5). This phrase already had a history: Charles Dickens had used it in 1859 to describe the new London University (Dickens, 1859), and Sydney Webb applied it to the London polytechnics in 1898 (Webb, 1898). It was to be heard again throughout the history of the University of East London.

THE FORERUNNERS IN ESSEX

When Essex County Council found itself the beneficiary of funds provided by the Technical Instruction Act, it invited grant applications for suitable technical education schemes. The Essex Field Club proposed to provide themselves with a museum and the county with technical instruction. (As we have just seen the club's collection ended up at the Passmore Edwards Museum).

The Field Club was an influential society whos interests lay in the study of 'the natural sciences.' Several of its members sat on Essex County Council. Some were scientists, including R Meldola, Professor of Chemistry at Finsbury Technical College; Professor William Flower, Director of the Natural History Museum; and Sir Henry E. Roscoe, Professor of Chemistry at Owen's College Manchester and a former member of the Royal Commission on Technical Instruction (*Essex Naturalist*, 1891, p264).

The county's initial share of 'whisky money' in 1891 amounted to over £16,000, which was distributed by a joint committee of six members of the field club and six from the county council, to local technical instruction committees (SE, 1891, p2). During 1891 some 22,807 people attended 580 separate classes throughout the County in subjects including agriculture, shorthand, drawing, nursing, and woodwork. Cookery classes accounted for over a quarter of the total. A year later 26,140 people had attended a total of 915 technical instruction classes (Nicholas, 1894, p48). Technical instruction classes were usually held in the evening. For the more remote villages, visiting instructors were provided, for other more populous areas provision was more comprehensive. Classes were either at convenient school premises and town halls or later at purpose built technical institutes at Southend-on-Sea (1895), Leyton (1896), Walthamstow (1897) and East Ham (1905).

During 1891 the committee also arranged courses for training elementary school teachers, so they might be qualified to give technical instruction in their own localities. Direct grants were given to the Essex Beekeepers' Association and the Essex Industrial School. A travelling dairy was organized.

With the 1902 Education Act, the county was divided into eighteen districts, which were largely coterminous with the Poor Law unions. Nine highly populated districts were classified under the Act as Part III authorities, which gave them responsibility for elementary education: they were the Boroughs of Chelmsford, Colchester, East Ham, Harwich, and Southend-On-Sea, and the Urban Districts of Barking, Ilford, Leyton and Walthamstow (Sadler, 1906, p20).

In 1905 the Essex Education Committee commissioned Michael E Sadler, Professor of the History and Administration of Education at Manchester University, to carry out a survey of secondary and higher education. Sadler's plan for technical education envisaged that the county should be serviced by three centres for what he termed 'higher technical work', providing day and evening classes;

> Across the County, in outline roughly a rectangle, the main line of the Great Eastern Railway runs diagonally. Along this line should be the chief centres of higher technical education. Two, West Ham and Chelmsford, already exist, a third is needed in Colchester, and the sequence will be complete. (Sadler, 1906, p76)

At Chelmsford there were the county laboratories and gardens, which concentrated on the agricultural sciences. The West Ham Technical Institute was actually outside the county, but it was well established by 1905, with the added appeal of internal degrees of the University of London in certain courses (see Chapter 5). It was also well situated, at Stratford, for easy access from Essex by rail. Sadler recommended that the county should make a contribution to the maintenance of the institute, proportional to the numbers of Essex students, and suggested that the county should have some representation on the institute's committee (Sadler, 1906, p76).

But it was at Colchester, in the northeast, where the provision of higher technical training was considered most inadequate. Here Sadler was reluctant to recommend the construction of a separate technical institute, on the grounds of cost. Instead he suggested that facilities at a grammar school should be improved, for joint use. Attempts to organize an institution in Colchester, based on the Colchester School of Art (established 1885), technical instruction classes and university extension lectures and aspiring to university college status, were frustrated by underfunding (Sadler, 1906, p253). A building housing a technical institute and art school was completed in 1912 (Brown, 1980, p68).

The technical institutes at Leyton, Walthamstow and Colchester each provided accommodation for day schools, which had been associated with the institutions since their construction, and were a common practice elsewhere. Those at Leyton and Walthamstow had been recognised as secondary schools in 1902, but later moved out, to be replaced by trade, or junior technical schools in 1916 and 1917 respectively. Boys were offered a three year course from the age of 12, combining a general education with the preparation for a career in industry (with an emphasis on engineering) or commerce (Lester Smith,

1928, p55). A similar commercial school for girls had also been established at Walthamstow in 1919.

In 1928 these institutions, along with the schools of art, offered nearly all the council's full time technical and art education. By this time the East Anglian Institute for agricultural education at Chelmsford had ceased to be the county's responsibility (Lester Smith, 1928, p58), and when East Ham and Southend-on-Sea acquired county borough status in 1915, and 1914 respectively, their technical colleges were also lost to the county. There were 200 full-time students, more or less, at each of the technical colleges in Colchester, Leyton and Walthamstow and at the Walthamstow Commercial School for girls: there were 40 or 50 back at the art schools at Chelmsford, Colchester and Leyton, at which there were also a large number of part-time students (Lester Smith, 1928, p55).

Evening classes were still the main provision for technical education within the county. At the 'evening institutes' in urban areas, a variety of courses could be pursued, including engineering, chemistry, architectural and building trades, languages and domestic and commercial subjects. The largest of these were in Leyton and Walthamstow, where the technical colleges were located, and enrolments in the rapidly expanding areas of Barking and Romford (which included Dagenham) showed a significant increase during the latter part of the 1920s (Lester Smith, 1928, p56).

On the other hand, courses in rural districts were in decline. In 1913 the number of classes was 116: in 1927 it had fallen to a mere 20 (Lester Smith, 1928, p57). A number of adult education courses were also organised, by the university extension boards and the Workers Educational Association. In 1928 at Barking these included musical appreciation, elocution and dramatic art, dramatic literature and elocution; at Leyton, nature study, modern social problems, English in speech and writing, local government, psychology, dramatic literature, and economics (Lester Smith, 1928, p59). Other voluntary organisations providing educational classes included the Women's Institute, which appeared to be most active in less metropolitan areas of the county, the Walthamstow Educational Settlement, and the Pettit Farm Settlement at Dagenham (EEC, 1935, p181-94).

By the 1920s the county's 19 districts were responsible for elementary education, and 15 of these also dealt with 'higher' education, that is secondary, technical and evening classes. There were 7 higher education district subcommittees, all subject to the general control of the county education committee. The growth of population and the existence of so many districts, each with a separate rating system, were increasingly thought to be hindering development (EEC, 1935, p11). At an annual general meeting of the Association of Technical Institutions in 1935, the county's Director of Education, John Sargent, said,

> It will be apparent that from whatever there might have been to say for such a system from the point of view of stimulating local patriotism, provision on any large scale, e.g., the building of a technical college, or for any considerable accession of population often led to local patriotism being tempered by financial considerations. (Sargent, 1935)

Throughout the 1920s, educational debate in Essex was dominated by housing developments on the outskirts of London. The London County Council's estate at Becontree faced the county council with the responsibility to provide schools. As early as December 1919 the authority estimated that educational facilities would be required for about 20,000 pupils in 20 elementary schools, two secondary schools, two continuation schools and one trade school:

They estimated the approximate capital costs of these schools at £725,000, the elementary schools accounting for £500,000. They also urged that the lay-out should provide land for schools free of cost to the Council, and that the LCC should contribute to the cost of erection. (LCC, 1920)

In December 1927 controversy over the cost of educational facilities at Becontree flared up again. The county council had found itself struggling to keep pace with the need for schools. They had apparently underestimated the scale of demand:

When the development of the estate was first under consideration, it was estimated that the school population would be from 1 to 1.25 per house, but up to the present moment it appears to have worked out at the rate of approximately 1.6 per house. (*Essex Chronicle*, 1927, p4)

The director of education reported later that while the national average was only about 1 child per house, on the Becontree estate it was expected to be not less than 1.5, and probably as high as 2.0 in places (Lester Smith, 1928).

By December 1927 the education committee had either erected or were planning schools to accommodate 20,672 children within the Becontree area, some of it in temporary accommodation (*Essex Chronicle*, 1927).

A flurry of letters passed between the chairman of the education committee, Alderman J H Burrows, and the President of the Board of Education, Lord Eustace Percy. The county council was concerned about its rural ratepayers, and sought more money from central government, which remained intransigent. Lord Eustace Percy refused to make Essex a special case, which drew an irate response from the education committee chairman:

Our whole case is that it is without parallel, different from any other movement of population that has taken place in England. It involves the transfer of about 130,000 people by one authority from its area into that of another. It is an organized exodus without industrial aspect. Its sole motive is residence, the creation by a public authority, pressed by H.M. Government, of a vast dormitory in an agricultural County. The responsibility for the scheme rests upon the Government; completely ignoring Essex, they rushed it through in their natural zeal for houses at all costs after the close of war. (*The Times*, 1928, p9)

The report for 1925-1928 demonstrated the education committee's preoccupation:

The provision of the necessary schools has occupied the attention of the Committee constantly throughout the period of this review, while they have been obliged to give much consideration to the serious financial problem resulting from the establishment of this dormitory town in their area. (EEC, 1928, p5)

One consequence, as the same report admitted, was that technical and adult education were inadequate:

A survey by the Trade, Technical and Art Schools Sub-Committee of the whole problem of Technical and Adult Education in the County appears to be an urgent necessity. It seems necessary to recapture some of the enthusiasm with which the Mechanics Institutes were established in the last century; to reconsider the whole framework of Technical Education in the County in the light of modern industrial requirements, and to explore fully the possibility of meeting more effectively the educational needs of the adolescent during the post-elementary years and of bringing, in conjunction with the Extra-Mural Boards of Universities, young men and women into contact with modern knowledge. (EEC, 1928, p65)

Between 1930 and 1931 the county reorganised higher (that is post-elementary) education. A new regional system was created, and four regional higher educa- tion sub-committees created. These were dominated by county members, but contained members from the Part III authorities, responsible for elementary education, and representatives of the district sub-committees.

The north-eastern region comprised Belchamp & Hal- stead, Lexden & Winstree, Tendring, and part of the Maldon and Braintree District Sub-Committee areas, as well as the Boroughs of Harwich and Colchester. Its population stood at 155,892 in 1931, and recent growth was said to have been mainly in the seaside towns of Frinton, Walton and Clacton. Industry was stable or even in decline (Sargent, 1935, p181).

The central region, described as a 'diagonal strip stretch- ing across the county from Saffron Walden to the outskirts of Southend, with its centre in Chelmsford' (Sargent, 1935), comprised Billericay, Dunmow, Saffron Walden & Stansted, and part of the Maldon and Braintree district sub- committee areas; as well as the borough of Chelmsford. Technical college buildings in Chelmsford (later to be known as Mid-Essex Technical College and School of Art and now part of Anglia Polytechnic University) had been extended in 1930, and a junior technical school added in 1933. The county borough of Southend also provided for the southernmost district of the region. The population of this region was 230,230 in 1931.

The south-western region, comprising the boroughs of Leyton and Walthamstow and the developing areas each side of Epping Forest (Chingford and Waltham Abbey in the west and Wanstead, Woodford, Chigwell and Epping on the east) was 'the only area in which provision for technical education was made on any considerable scale prior to 1931.' It contained the Victorian technical colleges at Leyton and Walthamstow, each with a resident junior technical school, as well as the Leyton School of Art and a junior commercial school for girls in Walthamstow. These facilities, which were claimed to be inadequate in 1935 – 'In the light of modern requirements perhaps the less said about the accommodation provided the better' (Sargent, 1935) – had already been criticised over thirty years before. In 1903 an editorial in the *Leyton and District Times* (1903) complained that the shortage of accommodation at Leyton Technical College had forced local children to be placed in neighbouring Walthamstow. More significantly Professor Sadler had also been critical of accommodation at the same institution two years later, in 1905 (Sadler, 1906, p130). The regional population was 380,275 in 1931 (Sargent, 1935).

The south-eastern region, comprising the Orsett, Rochford and Romford district sub-committee areas and the boroughs of Barking and Ilford, was a great swathe of southern Essex, which stretched eastwards along the Thames from Barking as far as the outskirts of Southend, in which all the heaviest concentrations of industry were located. The population of the region had more than doubled from 248,798 in 1921 to 530,000 by 1935 (Sargent, 1935).

SOUTH EAST ESSEX TECHNICAL COLLEGE
An early outcome of this regional reorganisation was a report on the provision of technical education in south west Essex in January 1931, which recommended two new technical colleges at Leyton and Barking (EEC, 1931a, p155). Within six months the national financial crisis had intervened. Among the economies in Essex

were 'the withdrawal of all building schemes for education, except those actually contracted for' (*The Times*, 1931, p6), the postponement of a scheme for a tunnel at Dartford and 'in view of the present emergency' of the Leyton technical college until 1933-4 (EEC, 1931b, p535). The college at Barking, however was to proceed in 1932-3 (Essex, 1931c, p769).

The year 1931 also saw a new director of education. John Sargent had been education officer for the county borough of Southend-on-Sea. Later, he was to be author of a report reorganising education in India, and to be given a knighthood. It was his vision which shaped the provision of the technical education in metropolitan Essex. He himself wrote, in 1938

> Essex, has conceived a quite new idea of the contribu-
> tion which a technical college can make to the life of
> the community. Previously the sort of education offered
> by a technical college was quite different in character
> and spirit from adult education in the accepted sense of
> that term. Nowadays the technical college is no longer
> merely a means of helping people to learn a little more
> about a subject they already know something of, just
> in order that they may earn a little more money.
> Education authorities are beginning to visualise the
> technical college as offering education in those arts by
> which all of us are able to live in unity, and as embracing
> within its curriculum anything which may be regarded
> as a proper subject of study for all men and women who
> support themselves. (Sargent, 1938)

In establishing its colleges Essex was self consciously a pioneer, following the principles of the Hadow Report of 1926. The earlier generation of technical institutes in Essex and elsewhere had been hosts to junior technical, trade or commercial schools. But in the new regional technical colleges in Essex pupils were to enter at the age of 11 and for the first two years receive an education similar to that in secondary schools, then in subsequent years take a series of optional courses in which non-academic courses would play an increasingly prominent part. A brochure issued by the education committee for the opening of the South East Essex Technical College described the new schools in the following terms:

> The schools will differ from secondary schools in not taking set examinations, and in allowing greater freedom of choice to both pupils and teachers, particularly in grouped courses incorporating the principles of technology, art and commerce. At the same time, they will differ from junior technical and commercial schools not only in the length of their courses, and the means by which the children are originally elected, but also in respect of the standard and nature of the instruction offered. Technical skill and manual dexterity will not be pursued as such; the object will be to cultivate an interest in the wider problems of modern industry rather than in the technical difficulties of particular processes, so that the pupil, upon entering employment, will bring to bear an interest in his trade or profession not confined only to the office or the workshop, but embracing its more comprehensive aspects, whether economic, technical or sociological. (SEET, 1936a)

The Board of Education had earlier rejected similar schemes elsewhere, but by 1935 was prepared to permit at Dagenham 'an experiment...which may have far reaching effects on the education system of the country' (Education, 1936, p549).

In 1939 a Government enquiry on secondary education (with special reference to grammar and technical high schools), led by Mr Will Spens, was recommending, technical high schools and seeking to raise their status.

The natural ambition of the clever child has been turned towards the grammar school and the professional occupations rather than towards the technical high schools and industry. Furthermore, there is the regrettable and undesirable difference in social esteem. We are concerned to secure and to emphasize the parity of all types of secondary school, but there is no point at which this is sociologically more important than in regard to the relative position of the grammar schools and the proposed technical high schools. (Spens, 1939, p274)

Since the south-eastern region was in a state of rapid development, and industry and population expected to grow still further, planners of technical education were faced with the problem of where to put a technical college to serve the region. Location was complicated by immediate needs, availability of land, and the 'present embryo stage of transport development'. A site of about 17 acres was acquired 'on the borders of Barking, Dagenham and Ilford, which is on or near the main arteries of traffic' (Sargent, 1935).

The foundation stone of the college was finally laid by Herwald Ramsbotham MP, parliamentary secretary to the Board of Education, on June 5 1935, with the comment that, 'large aggregations of capital and industry' had destroyed the old apprenticeship systems:

the burden of training the apprentices had largely been shifted from the shoulders of the employer to the State and the local education authority.

He called for more participation from industry and business men. Two weeks earlier, the Chancellor of the Exchequer had indicated that industry was having a problem recruiting a qualified workforce from among the unemployed.

Referring to the board of governors, Mr Ramsbotham

mentioned that the membership included representatives
of local industry, for example the Ford works' chief engineer, members of the county council, and members with
a special interest in education, including the former chief
inspector of the Board of Education's technical branch (*The
Times*, 1935, p10).

The local press was enthusiastic; '£200,000 Technical
College Is Nearly Ready', averred the *Dagenham Post*
(1936a). Its reporter was shown round the college by the
Principal, Mr Haler, on August 7th 1936. Accommodation
was for 1,000 day students and 5,000 evening students,
with work facilities which would 'enable students to
become anything from a model housewife to a qualified engineer'. The dining room was admired. 'It is a
quick lunch idea, popular in America.' Students would
collect their food from a long table by a serving hatch:
it was a cafeteria. The paper's report on the college's
inaugural dance called it a 'palace of learning' (Dagenham
Post, 1936b).

The college was opened on November 24, 1936 by
Oliver Stanley, President of the Board of Education. He
too spoke about the changing face of industry; there was
new competition from countries previously regarded as
'agricultural nations'. The highly-specialised nature of
industry required a workforce with a modern technical
education, and the geographical redistribution of industry.

> "I welcome this college." said Mr. Stanley, "on three
> grounds. By its very size it is one of the biggest under-
> takings of its kind yet seen. It represents cooperation
> on the art of many areas and many types of industry.
> Finally, it embodies experimental features particularly
> a new type of junior full-time school the success
> of which we shall watch with interest." (*The Times*,
> 1936, p9)

The college had five departments; art, commerce, science, domestic science and engineering. Another local paper, the *Ilford Recorder*, called it, in a headline, 'The Workers' University', noting in particular that swimming bath and gymnasium (as yet unbuilt) would cost an additional £28,000. Miss M. E. Tabor, chairman of the education committee, hoped

> that it will attract large numbers of the women and girls of this neighbourhood. Homemaking is by far the largest industry in this and other residential neighbourhoods, and I hope that women and girls will find real help towards the solution of their problems in the home. Their work is in many ways one on which the health and wellbeing of the country largely depends. (Ilford, 1936, p20)

She went on,

> Personally I would like to think of this College as a University for those who have to enter wage earning at a comparatively early age, and therefore are not able to continue the education which others more fortunate receive.... I would like to think that here they can have a good general education, the various means for qualifying in their careers, and the facilities for physical development, in fact all those advantages which the universities give. In the social life of this College they will find companionship and friendship among those of similar tastes. (*Dagenham Post*, 1936, p1)

As people were leaving the opening ceremony, and crowding into the corridor, all the lights on the ground floor fused. Attendants produced torches and current was restored in five minutes.

THE SOUTH WEST ESSEX TECHNICAL COLLEGE

The selection of a site for the South West Essex Technical College was similarly complicated by the need for accessibility to the public. Transport facilities were said to be well developed, but Epping Forest formed a wedge through the centre of the region. So the site finally chosen was in Forest Road, Walthamstow, and consisted of fields formerly belonging to Chestnuts Farm, where, it was said 'the main traffic routes both from the east and west of the forest converge' (Sargent, 1935).

The foundation stone was laid by county councillor Joseph Hewett, on 8th July 1937. When the Principal, H Lowery, arrived at the college in April 1938, the building was still incomplete: 'certain parts existed as a mere shell and the workshops in foundation line only' (SWETC, 1939a, pp45). Delay was blamed on the difficulty of obtaining materials and labour. Even so students enrolled for the following academic year, and the term began on October 3 (Bray, 1947, p9).

The official opening took place several months later on February 28 1939, by Earl De La Warr, President of the Board of Education. The event was captured by British Gaumont, a newsreel company. It was a brief 'roving camera' report, competing for attention with prospects for the Grand National, royal visits, fire at an asylum in Quebec and a review of the Spanish Civil War. The commentary began,

> This magnificent building is the South West Technical College and School of Art. Tall, broad and stately.... We show you one or two glimpses of the well equipped interior. Already 5,000 students have enrolled for the first session, which may be an encouragement to other large towns to build likewise. (Gaumont, 1939)

Indeed enrolment in October, particularly for evening

classes, had been so successful that an accommodation crisis existed before the institution had even officially opened. Evening classes attracted 5,802 students, 2,337 more than had attended similar courses at the constituent Walthamstow and Leyton institutions in the previous year. During that first term senior classes were temporarily held at the Sir George Monoux Grammar School, and later that academic year the old commercial school and technical college premises in Hoe Street were reoccupied (SWETC, 1939a). A member of staff would later write, that 'only for the first day or two of its existence has the whole complex organisation been housed under one roof' (Bray, 1947, p90).

'Earl De La Warr Opens £240,000 Technical College' was the main headline to an article in the *Walthamstow, Leyton and Chingford Guardian*. Others were 'People's University And Community Centre' and 'Demand Has Already Overflowed Capacity'. Miss Tabor, the Chairman of the education committee

> hoped the 25 years upon which they had just embarked would be remarkable for its technical education, and they had endeavoured to make a start in Essex. Their policy was to make the sphere of education and opportunity as wide as possible.

Alderman Percy Astins, chairman of the governing body described the college as 'a great people's university' and 'the vision of John Sargent'. Another alderman, Joseph Hewett, said that he knew of people who had claimed Essex were being a little too extravagant. One person had publicly described the technical college in Dagenham as Buckingham Palace No 2. (WLCG, 1939). In the official programme the Principal wrote,

> Industrialism has heralded a mechanical age which in its turn has resulted in the release of the worker from

the bondage of his daily task and provided him with
time for relaxation and recreation recreation .... A new
problem of training has thus arisen it becomes necessary
to provide for training for leisure as well as for vocation
and there are certain educationalist who do not doubt
that the former is of even greater importance than the
latter. (SWETC, 1939b)

The college's departments were engineering, science,
industrial and fine art, architecture and building, commerce, languages and social studies, domestic science and a
women's department. All courses were to be open equally
to women and men. The women's department provided
some afternoon sessions for mothers, and a nursery was
provided for children.

"The task," added Lord de La Warr, "of building up
a skilled healthy and intelligent body of workers is
equally important for war or peace. No victory however
complete, will enable us to survive as a great power if
we lack it. And if as we all hope, there is no war, then
the normal rivalries that already existed between nations
will continue, and it will be by this standard that both
nations and their systems of government be judged".
(*Essex Chronicle*, 1939)

Six months later Britain declared war on Germany. The
technical high schools were evacuated, and the Essex technical colleges played host to the military. At Walthamstow,
for example, training courses were provided for the British
Army, ATS, Royal Navy and Royal Air Force. By 1945
some 12,000 service personnel had passed through the
college. For civilians, evening classes at the institution
were rendered impractical by wartime conditions, and
switched to weekends. Day work continued very much
as before (Bray, 1947).

CHAPTER 4
College and Community

The colleges which came to make up the University of East London were founded by local authorities to serve their own areas. As the economy and population of London moved eastwards in the nineteenth century new local government structures were established, and the new county borough of West Ham created, as one of its first acts, a new technical institute. The eastward movement of population continued in the 1920s and 1930s, in 'ribbon development' and as planned by the London County Council. The response of the county of Essex was to build two impressive technical colleges to serve their localities as part of a county-wide system.

However, the question of how institutions of further and higher education relate to their localities proved more problematic than those first policy decisions assumed. In the predecessor colleges, in the Polytechnic (see chapter 6) and in the University, there were and are tensions between service to localities and the facts of student mobility, between the needs of local industry and commerce and academic concern for the subject, the students and the institution. When the Polytechnic was formed, in 1970, on multiple sites, these tensions were complicated: the colleges' relations with their communities came also to involve the Polytechnic's relations within itself as a community, raising questions of how far its 'dispersal' was a problem, how far an opportunity.

NINETEENTH CENTURY ROOTS AND TWENTIETH CENTURY PLANNING

In the early years at the West Ham Technical Institute the students were predominantly from the county borough. When, for example, 1,595 students enrolled for the first year, three quarters of them (1194) lived within West Ham. The largest groups of student occupations were categorised as: women engaged at home 376, engineering trades 305, building trades 304, commercial pursuits 296 and teachers 152. The Principal noted the following year that:

> The statistics show in a very gratifying way that the institute is being largely used by people for whom it is intended, namely, those earning their living by some trade or profession... this year a far larger proportion of students have joined from the southern part of the Borough, and, owing to the way in which residents have taken up the classes, we have had to altogether refuse admission to outside students in many of our classes, so that the proportion of students living and working outside the Borough will be even less that it was last year. (West Ham, 1899, p644)

Early prospectuses declared:

> The Institute classes are open to students of both sexes, no matter what may be their place of residence or employment, but preference is given to those residing or employed within the County Borough of West Ham. (WHTI, 1899)

During the first half of the twentieth century, it served a spectrum of local needs for technical education. It took school-age pupils from the county borough in its junior technical school of engineering (1913), junior school of commerce (1936), and of art (1916), girls' trade school (1913), and junior school of building (1942). 'Senior work' for students beyond school age (which would now be called 'further education') was offered mainly in the form of evening classes or day classes in technical, commercial and art education. These classes attracted students from outside the county borough: in 1938 (these figures exclude art) the percentage of evening students from the county borough was 60 per cent: 31 of the 41 full-time students, but only 17 of the 94 part-time day students lived in the county borough (HMI, 1938a).

From 1920 the system of fees erected barriers to students from outside West Ham, though arrangements were made with neighbouring authorities. In 1925, for example, day students from East Ham were charged 50 per cent over those from West Ham, and those from other authorities were charged double. Evening students from East Ham paid the same as those from West Ham, those from London paid 50 per cent more, and others paid double (WHMC, 1925). However, 'free trade' agreements were reached with neighbouring authorities, and by 1938 students from East Ham, London, Middlesex and Essex could enrol on full-time and part-time courses at the ordinary fee (HMI 1938). Local students were encouraged by scholarships and studentships, initially relying to a considerable extent on philanthropy from bodies such as the Stratford Cooperative Society, Thames Iron Works, Great Eastern Railway Mechanics Institute, Mr W Duncan Knight JP and the Mayor. The council increased its support: in the first session it offered about 30 scholarships (WHTI, 1899); by 1920 its scheme made awards to 120 day students, waiving fees and supporting 80 of them with maintenance funds, and also providing 140 evening students with small sums towards books and instruments (HMI, 1921).

A productive relationship with local industry and commerce was aspired to in principle but never satisfactorily resolved in practice. In 1906 a conference was held with eleven local manufacturing companies, the West Ham Trades Council and the education committee of the Stratford Co-operative Society, with the purpose of tailoring the work of the Institute to meet the needs of local industry, for which their co-operation was sought. The principal made a number of suggestions as to how this might be achieved. For day courses he suggested allowing company employees with particular skills or expertise to attend the Institute during the day time, in order to give instruction to the day students; engaging as employees at favourable rates those who had gone through approved day courses of study; granting facilities to teachers and students to visit their works; and allowing students to spend time at their works as part of their course of study. For evening classes he proposed refunds of fees for those who had done well, loans and gifts of books, excuse from overtime, and prizes given by Masters' Federation by those who did best (West Ham, 1906, p961). E G Howarth, head of residence of a Trinity College, Oxford, Mission and co-opted member of the Technical Institute Sub-Committee wrote of the meeting later:

> It was suggested by some members of the Committee that manufacturers might arrange for their apprentices or learners to attend the Institute during the ordinary hours of work, but this suggestion was not favourably received. (Howarth and Wilson, 1907, p327)

But the problems were not only those of interest or goodwill among educationists and industrialists. The nature of industry in West Ham was not predisposed to further education. Unlike many large provincial towns to which West Ham may have been compared, the economy of the borough was not dependent upon one major industry, and a considerable proportion of the working population was working outside the borough, either in London or neighbouring East Ham and Essex. The HMI Report of 1921 commented:

> the exceptionally high proportion of outworkers living in the Borough, and the miscellaneous and scattered nature of the local industries, differentiate West Ham from provincial cities of similar size in the matter of the possibilities of organised co-operation between schools and workshops. (HMI, 1921, p1)

Moreover, a large proportion of labour required for dock related work was unskilled and employed on a casual basis. Of the larger employers within the borough, with the exception of the Great Eastern Railway Company,

> there does not appear to be any one firm in West Ham employing a large amount of skilled labour. Much important skilled work is done in numerous small workshops. (HMI, 1921, p1)

There was also a recognised problem of co-ordination:

> A scheme with the object of bringing the Institute into touch with the firms in which the bulk of its students work would have to include manufacturing and trading concerns scattered all over London. In theory the object of a technical school is to provide instruction in connection with the employment of local ratepayers and their dependents, irrespective of place of employment. But it does seem that there should be a specially close relationship between the

trades and manufactures actually carried on in a town and the local technical school, and the absence of any definite scheme for furthering such relationship in the case of West Ham is somewhat anomalous. (HMI, 1921, p1)

It was also noted that the technical institute's governors were at that time a higher education sub-committee of the education committee. Its members were chiefly council-lors, with a minority of co-opted members:

from their method of appointment they cannot be said to be closely in touch with the skilled trades for which the school makes provision. (HMI, 1921, p2)

HMI advocated the appointment of advisory committees, especially in connection with the girls' trade school and building classes (HMI, 1921, p20). They also noted, however, a conflict between university level work and senior 'technological' work:

All that needs to be said here is that work of this latter kind, in close connection with industry, has a real and proper place in any important technical institution. At present, partly for lack of accommodation, no great attempt is being made in West Ham to foster it. It is to be hoped that its claims will not be permanently disregarded. (HMI, 1921, p19)

In 1933 the Board of Education inquired into relations between technical education and industry and commerce, and responding to HMI's request for information Principal Baillie commented:

Local firms have always been willing to supply us with information wanted for specific purposes, or distribute our prospectuses or do anything short of expending money.

He was able to provide only a few items of evidence: £15 in scholarships from the National Association of Master Bakers and Confectioners, a motor engine presented by Morris of Oxford, a Chingford firm giving day-release to their apprentices for classes in optics, many local firms paying fees of evening students, one general conference with employers and several special conferences with particular trades (Baillie, 1933). To these instances could be added evening classes for employees of cooperative societies and courses in industrial chemistry (HMI, 1938a) which had been established after a survey of local employers (West Ham, 1938, p149).

In fact, the West Ham college related to London, rather than just the county borough of West Ham. Thus, the junior technical school for girls contained 77 pupils in 1927, and was described as only one of two schools in the country which offered a three year training in dressmaking for business purposes:

> West Ham supplies many of the workers in the West End of London needle trades and as Dressmaking is one of the largest of women's skilled trades there need be no anxiety about their being absorbed into the trade if a larger number received the training. (BOE, 1927)

A major attempt by the county borough to make the Institute part of its educational provision for the community was the production in 1920 of an education plan in response to the Education Act, 1918. Two years after the end of the Great War, the borough contained about 294,000 people. Of these, 61,700 were children between the ages of 5 and 14, attending 64 publicly maintained schools. Most left school at this stage or even earlier, for only about 200 a year went into secondary schooling at the age of 11, and even smaller numbers went later into the borough's two higher elementary, or junior technical schools. For those who left after compulsory elementary education, seven evening schools provided a way to continue their studies, though annual enrolments had never exceeded 3,500, and many who enrolled dropped out before completing their courses (West Ham, 1920). Recruitment to the Municipal Technical Institute came from the evening and secondary schools, and other unspecified institutions (which would have included the Mechanics Institute, and those outside the borough). The numbers were described merely as 'a small stream', while those proceeding directly from secondary school to university were 'a trickle' (West Ham, 1920).

The 1918 Act, passed before the Great War was over, effectively made schooling compulsory until the age of 14, and permitted local authorities to raise the leaving age to 15, or provide day-continuation schools one day a week for youths between the ages of 14 and 16 years. The Act also offered the prospect of a modified grants system that would ensure a 50 per cent Government subsidy for all approved expenditure on education (Barnard, 1947, pp271-3; Stevenson, 1991, p248). Local education authorities were invited by Board of Education Circular 1096 to prepare and submit to the board comprehensive plans for their local schemes:

> [the authority] ... shall not take too short a view, or confine its educational vision within the limits which present resources in personnel, material or money may suggest. (BOE, 1918)

Encouraged by government to prepare an all embracing scheme, West Ham optimistically proposed 'free full-time education for all to the age of sixteen', to be achieved within the following fifteen years. Within two years 12,000 elementary school leavers would attend the proposed part-time continuation schools, and numbers at secondary schools would be doubled. There would also be 'central schools' similar to secondary provision, but initially without the higher work. More than 600 extra teachers would be required.

Such a drastic improvement in the local system was expected to create a large increase in demand for what was then called 'higher education':

> A real interest in some line of study or of craft will have been fostered in many young citizens, and every opportunity should be given to them to pursue it. (West Ham, 1920)

The Municipal Technical Institute, flagship of civic endeavour, existed for such a purpose and was the borough's centre of excellence in higher education. It would expand accordingly. The junior technical schools, residents of the Institute, were to be phased out, their narrow vocational training considered inappropriate for students under the age of sixteen. This would release space for the expansion of more advanced work. The school of art, the secretarial and domestic science departments would continue, and new courses in different subjects be provided as demands dictated. A new department would be specifically developed to provide specialised training to teachers of art, domestic subjects, handicrafts and physical training, for whom scholarships would be provided.

As for the most advanced work in the Institute, 'internal' science and engineering degrees were still being awarded by the University of London (see Chapter 5). Similar degree courses were to be developed in economics, social science and the arts as soon as practicable, 'with the intention of claiming for the institution the position of a constituent College of the University, serving a wider district than West Ham' (West Ham, 1920).

Alas in 1921 a Parliamentary Committee on national expenditure, under the chairmanship of Sir Eric Geddes, recommended that grants to education should be reduced by about a third. The 'Geddes Axe' led to some drastic economies in education. The borough kept up its spirits with an 'education week' of pageantry, poetry, sport, open-air concerts and even a competition to model the mayor's head, while a specially commissioned film celebrated the breadth of West Ham's educational achievements (*Daily News*, 1922). But in the end the Municipal Technical Institute got nothing but a new name; it became the Municipal College.

Nor was it effectively integrated into a local system. For example HMI reported in 1938:

> The relation of the Evening Institutes to the Municipal College is rather a slender one, and apart from some students who pass on to higher work, the institutes cannot be regarded as feeders to the college. They seem to continue their work in splendid isolation, and as they are administered separately there seems to be little to bind them to what should be for them the parent institution influencing and inspiring their work.... Superintendents of evening institutes have mentioned cases of students passing on to the college, but later returning to the institute to continue their studies. (HMI, 1938b)

The industrial and commercial environments of the two Essex colleges were very different from that of West Ham. West Ham had developed on the triumphalism of nineteenth century industrial expansion, and gloried in its municipal achievements – capped by a college that was almost a university. In Essex, however, the regional technical colleges were planned as part of a county infrastructure. The role of these colleges was supposed to be complementary to their relative catchment areas.

When John Sargent, the director of education for Essex, spoke before the Association of Technical Institutions in 1935 he explained that in the rapidly developing south-eastern region of the county 'it was very difficult to forecast how far the incoming population should be regarded as a dormitory one or as seeking employment within the region itself'. While there were already a number of substantial industries in the region (varying from photographic and printing works at Ilford, to margarine, cement and oil factories along the banks of the Thames), the end of industrial expansion was by no means in sight. Ford's works at Dagenham and the Bata shoe factory at Tilbury, for example, had yet to reach their contemplated maximum development:

> The primary problem, therefore, has been to decide for which of the industries in the region the proposed College should cater.... (Sargent, 1935)

In the south-western region, however, there was no such prospect of industrial developments on any comparative scale:

> There are, of course, important works in connection with the railways, gas industry and other forms of engineering, but the bulk of the prospective students will be engaged in a great variety of industrial and commercial occupations outside the area, and above all in London. (Sargent, 1935)

Looking back on the foundation of the Walthamstow college, the chairman of governors, Percy Astins, who had been involved since its inception, recalled the geographical case in 1955:

it having been visualized that, unlike colleges situated in heavy industrial areas, the South West College would serve only the secondary industries for which design and the humanities (including arts and crafts) were of the greatest importance. This policy had been accepted by the then Board of Education and it was for this particular reason that the Leyton School of Art, which had hitherto been an independent unit from the technical college, had been absorbed within the general functional structure of this College; thus, full recognition of such policy was established even before the College came into being. (SWETC, 1955)

Students were mostly local, from the catchment areas planned for regions within Essex. Of the earliest intake at the South West Essex Technical College in 1938-39, only 515 students out of a total of 5,822 (or 9 per cent of senior students for whom details were known) were classified as being from 'other districts': these included Ilford, Forest Gate, Stratford, and Tottenham, as well Epping which was within the south west region (SWETC, 1939a). Figures from 1948-9 show that the residence of the post-war student population had begun to change: 77 per cent were from the original catchment area, 13 per cent were from other areas 'in-county', and 11 per cent were 'out-county' (SWETC, 1949).

    Earliest available statistics for South East Essex Technical College students' place of residence illustrate its local function. In February 1948, 95 per cent were living in the original South East Essex catchment area defined by the county's regional pre-war plans: the boroughs of Ilford, Barking, Romford, and Dagenham; the urban districts of Hornchurch and Thurrock; the south east Essex division (SEETC, 1948a). These figures exclude enrolments for the technical school and make an interesting contrast to those for SWETC. There, in 1938 almost half of the 5,750 evening students (48.3 per cent) worked in London and slightly less than a third (32.3 per cent) worked in Essex. A decade later the situation was little changed: London 44.8, Essex 33.7 (SWETC, 1939a, 1949).

The most durable of the links made by the South East Essex Technical College with local industry began during its inaugural year. In 1936 there were 48 students attending 'Ford's classes' (SEETC 1936b). The company's scholarship plan, described in 1937, was intended to 'equip the student with the necessary experience and efficiency to ensure his competence and ability in all phases of automobile engineering, including a thorough understanding of the business, trade, and executive work appropriate to the student's future career.'

Nearly 50 technical colleges and schools across the United Kingdom were said to be participating in the scheme (SEETC, 1937). By 1939 there were 111 scholarship students at the South East Essex Technical College alone (SEETC, 1939), and when the company reorganised its training scheme in 1945 it agreed to broaden the scope of its training so that national certificate and other academic courses could be included (SEETC, 1945).

The South West Essex Technical College opened its doors barely a year before the country was at war, and its local linking had to wait until the 1940s.

POST-WAR RECONSTRUCTION

After World War II the situation of the colleges changed utterly. The structures of education were rebuilt by the Education Act 1944. It created a system of secondary education administered by local education authorities, which came to encompass grammar, secondary modern and technical high schools The junior technical schools of West Ham were quickly separated off into new technical high schools. The technical high schools at Barking and Walthamstow had to wait until 1960 and 1958 respectively

(BRCT, undated, SWETC, 1959). The Act also created a post-school system by defining 'further education' and by requiring LEAs to secure 'adequate facilities' in their areas and to draw up 'schemes' of further education.

Meanwhile, the demobbed troops were looking to make up for lost opportunities and seeking education, particularly courses at degree and professional levels, encouraged by the government's Further Education and Training Scheme, which offered financial support (Lowe, 1988, p63). There were many more potential students than the universities could accommodate, and colleges within the further education system were encouraged to meet the demand. Numbers in further education more than doubled: full-time students numbers increased from 20,000 in 1937-8 to 45,000 in 1946-7, and part-time day from 89,000 to 200,000 (White Paper, 1956). Within this expansion, numbers studying 'advanced' courses, that is degrees, HND-HNC and equivalent professional qualifications became a larger proportion of the whole.

The expansion had its impact on our colleges. At Barking nine students were awarded science degrees in 1946-7, 28 in 1949-50; 21 were awarded HNCs in 1946-7, 40 in 1949-50; one RIBA Final part one, and five Intermediate awards in 1946-7, but 10 Intermediate RIBA and five Final awards in 1949-50 (SEETC, 1948b, 1951a). At Walthamstow 15 BScs were awarded in 1946-7, 50 in 1949-50; 47 HNCs in 1946-7, 80 in 1949-50; two intermediate RIBA in 1946-7, increasing to 14 intermediate and two finals in 1948-49 (SWETC, 1947, 1948b, 1949). At West Ham 24 BScs were awarded in 1946-7, 31 in 1949-50; 13 HNCs and five HNDs in 1946-7, as compared to 27 HNCs in 1949-50 (WHMC, 1947, 1950).

Advisory committees, constituted from members of local companies, governors, professional or statutory bodies, became a feature of our colleges during the post-war era. At South East Essex Technical College in 1953 for example, committees existed for building, applied science, architecture and surveying, printing and allied crafts, engineering, commercial and professional studies, bakery studies (SEETC, 1954a). Some were less successful than others. In 1946, a plastics advisory committee at the South West Essex Technical College was inspired by the Percy Report to establish a plastics research centre at the college. But these ambitions were never fully realised. At a meeting in November 1948, when not a single industrial member had actually attended, it was noted that 'very little co-operation had been shown by the local plastics firms in encouraging their employees to attend classes' (SWETC, 1948a).

Similarly the 1947-8 annual report commented upon their lack of success:

> Unfortunately the number of students taking plastics has not reached expectations as apparently the industry continues to require mainly unskilled labour together with a few technicians who have had training up to the standard of the Higher National Certificate in Mechanical Engineering. (SWETC, 1948b)

The Committee was finally discontinued in 1949, and the laboratory utilised for chemical engineering (SWETC, 1949).

Sometimes the combined efforts of college and local companies were confounded by the very sectors of the local community that they were committed to help. As representatives of the South West Essex Technical College's technical and training advisory committee discovered in 1956:

> approaches made to certain secondary grammar schools by representatives of industry with regard to tech-

nical training had been totally rejected or ignored. (SWETC, 1956b)

Sandwich courses were an innovation welcomed by our colleges and local companies in the 1950s, for they offered the student 'layers' of full-time college experience alternated with industrial experience, over a number of years. The sandwich principle was by no means new to technical education, since the first sandwich courses had been tried out at the Royal Technical College, Glasgow in the 1880s, and at Sunderland Technical College in 1903 (Venables, 1955, p60, p86). Indeed Venables listed 36 colleges providing a range of courses in 1955 (Venables, 1955, pp623-5).

When the Government's 1956 White Paper and Circular 305 established a hierarchy within the technical college system, it was apparent that sandwich courses were expected to become the preserve of those at the top. Chiefly the CATs and 'a moderate number of (regional) colleges, which will have to be selected with the distribution of both industry and population in mind' (Burgess & Pratt, 1970, p40). Thus sandwich courses were not only educationally useful, but also a desirable acquisition for ambitious institutions.

At SEETC, there had been encouraging discussions with the Plessey Co Ltd, and Esso Petroleum about a whole range of proposed courses in 1955, and Ford were pressing for a sandwich course during the next session (SEETC, 1956a). Despite the reservations of the regional advisory council, a four year course covering mechanical and production engineering was started in 1956. In attendance were 77 Ford students, 43 of which had completed the first or second years of the scholarship courses, and 15 others from the Shell Refining Co, Plessey Co Ltd, Thames Board Mills and the Central Electricity Authority (SEETC, 1956d).

Proposals for a similar course in light current electrical engineering were vetoed by the Ministry of Education, despite the promise of 8 students from Plessey Co, and £1000 worth of new equipment, donated by Plessey 'as a token of goodwill' (SEETC, 1956). It was this particular course that Dr Heathcoat, the principal, had expected to develop into a prestigious Diploma of Technology course most easily (SEETC, 1956). But the prospective Plessey students were lost to Northampton Polytechnic in London (now the City University) (SEETC, 1957). Nevertheless by 1960 some 233 students were attending engineering or other sandwich courses at the College (SEETC, 1961).

At West Ham that same year, a five year sandwich course in chemical engineering which led to the college associateship was introduced, followed in 1961 by a three year course leading to a higher national diploma in applied physics (WHCT, 1962).

Meanwhile South West Essex Technical College was faced with postponing plans to establish a constructional engineering sandwich course in 1956, due to a disappointing response from students (SWETC, 1956). However by 1964 the principal was able to assert confidently, that while the college had only one sandwich course in operation, in civil engineering, this kind of course was

a distinctive feature of technical education which finds no parallel in the universities.

Highlighting one of the fundamental problems of assessing the constituent colleges' links with local industry and commerce, he wrote,

What figures cannot show is the close relationship which many members of the teaching staff, from Heads of Departments down, have with training and personnel officers and senior executives in commercial and industrial concerns over a wide area. (SWETC, 1964)

SITUATION AND STATUS

In the years following World War II the Government struggled to formulate policy for further education, particularly for 'advanced further education' (AFE – which would become, over the years, identified as 'higher education'). The Percy Report (1945) and subsequently the White Paper, 1951, recognised that some colleges in the FE system had a role alongside universities in producing professional engineers and technologists. As a result of the White Paper West Ham was in 1954 included among a select group of 24 technical colleges recognised under Circular 255, out of a total of 89 for which applications were submitted (Venables, 1955, p607), for national funding with 75 per cent grants for capital and running costs of advanced courses. As the Government developed its policies, however, a ruling principle emerged relating the level of colleges to their geographical coverage, and the White Paper of 1956 created eight, later ten, 'colleges, of advanced technology' as national institutions, and below them a hierarchy of regional, area and local colleges. The Government reasoned that it would be a more economical use of resources to concentrate advanced full-time and sandwich courses in a limited number of colleges which would attract students from a region, not just locally.

West Ham was designated in the first group of regional colleges, following the 1956 White Paper, but the Barking and Walthamstow colleges were not. The case for South East Essex Technical College received formidable support from local industry, and as the argument unravelled the threads of the Government's policy became clearer: the Government wanted selected colleges to concentrate on advanced work, and that implied not only expanding advanced work but also contracting and shedding lower level work.

In the light of the 1956 Government White Paper, Sir Patrick Hennessy, deputy chairman and managing director of the Ford Motor Company, wrote to the county chief education officer. He expressed the company's disappointment that South East Essex Technical College had not been included among the original 24 colleges to receive the 75 per cent grant for advanced work, noting that the White Paper indicated that there might be few additions to the list.

> We are proud of our College – of its great progress, and the fact that it has such an important place in a great industrial area,

wrote Hennessy, complimenting the institution for its 'foresight' in planning and developing sandwich courses. He went on,

> As you know, our Company is undertaking a huge expansion programme and this includes considerably increased facilities for technical education. Our plans, in a large part, will be closely tied to the South East Essex Technical College and its future – especially with regard to the proposed 'sandwich' courses. We are, therefore, expecting that the necessary facilities for advanced studies such as are envisaged in the White Paper will be made available at this College. (Hennessy, 1956)

Hennessy, who represented a major manufacturing company with a workforce of 45,000, expected the substance of his letter to be passed on to the Ministry.

Similarly, the training and education officer of the Plessey Company Ltd, wrote to say that his company wished to participate in the sandwich courses being established at SEETC. Plessey management were considering centralising their sandwich apprenticeship scheme on their Ilford factory, which held out the prospect of students' coming from as far afield as Swindon, Northampton and Rotherham. Since the White Paper had intimated that the bulk of full-time and sandwich courses should be carried out in colleges which concentrated on advanced courses, it would be appropriate for SEETC to be added to the list (SEETC, 1956b).

The principal, Dr Heathcoat, recommended that the college should begin to shed elementary day work to day release centres and evening institutes, including City & Guilds courses up to intermediate level and the first and second year stages of National Certificate courses. It had been pointed out to him 'privately on several occasions' by HM Inspectors that if SEETC was to be recognised as an advanced college, the secondary technical school would have to be housed in separate premises as soon as possible. He also recommended that 'we must do everything possible to increase the amount of research carried on within the College', and that they must continue to try and attract highly qualified staff. He described a

> great feeling of despondency among staff at the pros-
> pect that some advanced work will disappear to other
> Regional Colleges in the London area. It is incredible
> that in this important industrial area the College should
> not be given Regional status. The quality of staff must
> not be allowed to deteriorate. (SEETC, 1957b)

Essex made applications to the Ministry for regional status, but to no avail. The reason given by the Ministry was that the proportion of advanced work was not sufficiently high. At the 1956-7 SEETC prize giving ceremony Dr Heathcoat complained bitterly that the total volume of advanced work at the college was as high that at some of the regional colleges, and that the college output of graduates in past years had, in fact, been greater than that of some of the advanced colleges:

> The Ministry's answer to these points is that our
> proportion of advanced work is not high enough.

This reply has created dissatisfaction among the staff. It is precisely because we have carried out the Ministry's policy in the region and opened our doors to a variety of work, including less advanced work, to serve the needs of the region, that we are now refused status that we had expected. Moreover the reply is based on the false premise that advanced work and elementary work cannot flourish side by side. It also puts a dangerous premium on advanced courses to the disparagement of other courses when both are needed at this time. There is a growing feeling that it has been a great mistake to grade colleges in this manner, and that it will have an adverse effect on the recruitment of highly qualified staff to the great majority of technical colleges at this time of expansion. However, if colleges are to be graded it is important that we should achieve the status to which we have aspired.

There has also been a disquieting tendency in this area to attempt to concentrate more advanced work in a few London colleges in spite of the movement of population outwards. An example of this occurred in the discussion we had with the Regional Advisory Council in provision of courses in Lithography in our new printing extensions. This and similar cases have produced strong protests from the Governors and the Education Committee. (SEETC, 1957)

In 1961 the Minister of Education was reported to have accepted that the South East Essex Technical College had a *prima facie* case for regional designation. But he was concerned about the proximity of the college to West Ham College of Technology, which had already been designated. Similar claims for South West and Mid Essex technical colleges had been dismissed (SEETC, 1961a).

Circular 3/61 announced the Minister's intention of

revising the list. Ministerial re-appraisal of regional college status in the London and Home Counties region jeopardised two institutions. Brixton School of Building was considered to be providing too narrow a technological range of advanced courses, while West Ham College of Technology was under threat of being replaced by South East Essex Technical College:

> There appears to the Minister to be *prima facie* case for the designation of the South East Essex Technical College at Dagenham, and this raises the question ... whether, as a matter of good regional planning, there is a place for Regional Colleges at Dagenham and West Ham. As between the two colleges there is no doubt that the preference should be given to the South East Essex. The volume of advanced work there is now considerably greater than at West Ham, and West Ham also suffers from the serious handicap of accommodation which is quite inadequate for a Regional College. (MOE, 1961)

In West Ham it was recognised that nothing would be gained from arguing the West Ham case by making comparisons with its rival college, but that a case should be made for the logic of two regional colleges in the area, rather than just one (Vincent, 1961). Principal Bulmer also pressed for the purchase of adjacent land owned by the Territorial Army, emphasising the need for extra accommodation (Bulmer, 1961).

Meanwhile, Essex had drawn the principals of the West Ham and East Ham colleges into discussing the creation of a college of advanced technology (CAT). In 1962 a confidential report prepared by the county education officer, 'Technical Education in Metropolitan Essex', claiming informal Ministry approval, proposed the establishment of a new CAT on a site at Barley Lane,

Goodmayes, which would leave the existing colleges with only the lower level work. The report considered that the – then impending – regional recognition of SEETC presented no problem to the establishment of the CAT nearby, speculating that regional status could probably be transferred from the south east to the south west college, once the CAT was ready to operate (EEC, 1962). The SEETC Governors supported the principle of the report, by ten to one (SEETC, 1962a).

A few months later SEETC was granted regional college status (without West Ham losing), with the following ministerial proviso:

The Minister had made it clear that the decision was taken within the framework of existing policy and without prejudice to any recommendations the Committee on Higher Education, which is expected to report next year, might make as to the structure of Higher Education in general or the category of Regional Colleges in particular. In this connection the Minister was aware of the proposal for the new College of Technology at Ilford (SEETC, 1962b).

In May 1964 the college changed its name to the South East Essex College of Technology (SEETC, 1964).

THE REGION AND THE WORLD
The basis of regional planning for advanced students was flawed in a major respect – there were not in the 1950s sufficient advanced students from the region to sustain the courses. The immediate post-war boom proved short-lived. The demand from ex-service men and women was met, and by the beginning of the 1950s the advanced courses developed to meet their needs were running short of students. However, these courses were valued by the staff and, as noted above, were justified by national policy.

Faced with declining applications, the colleges turned to attract new students, particularly from overseas, and the continuation of advanced courses was sustained by these overseas students.

In all three colleges in the early 1950s declining numbers of advanced students had caused continuing anxiety. In 1954 SEETC's principal, Dr Heathcoat, warned that numbers of degree students might continue to drop: he noted that there were only five full-time students taking final degrees in biological subjects, although there were three specialist staff.

In 1955 the chief education officer of Essex, intimating that his suggestions emanated from the Ministry of Education, wrote to the colleges about low attendances on full-time courses. In 1956 the county education committee found that the future of the BSc special chemistry, BSc special physics and chef's courses at the South West Essex Technical College and the surveying course at the South East Essex Technical College were in doubt. It decided that they should 'continue for so long as arrangements can be made to combine suitable classes', and robustly 'adhered to the principle that full-time degree courses, especially BSc General Degree, are appropriately conducted in Technical Colleges, and in the view of the urgent need for technologists and scientists, hoped to see these courses developed.... The centralisation of full-time courses in London, which would be accentuated by the closing of such courses in colleges on the outskirts, was undesirable.' The courses were at continual risk of closure in the ensuing two years (SEETC, 1956e).

The main increase in overseas students began in the late 1950s (Soar, 1966). In 1950 the principal at West Ham had been authorised by the education committee to allow in 12 'colonial students' provided they did not deprive West Ham students of places. The question of fees needed settling, and from 1955 the authority was allowed to claim for such students though the 'out county' charge from the central 'pool' (Soar, 1966).

In 1953 almost half the 140 full-time day students were from overseas. Only 23 per cent were normally resident in West Ham and 14 per cent in Essex. In 1964 overseas students represented 48 per cent of all enrolments (total 1003) for full-time and sandwich courses at advanced level. Students from West Ham and East Ham represented a combined figure of just 4 per cent. Throughout engineering courses as a whole the overseas students accounted for 76 per cent (WHCT, 1964).

South West Essex Technical College received overseas students for various technical courses through the Colonial Office. In 1955 there were 113 overseas students out of a full-time total of 724, from 29 different countries, including Nigeria 26, Gold Coast 22 and Kenya 7 (SWETC, 1956a). In 1963, overseas students accounted for 24 per cent of the full-time and sandwich, and 8 per cent of part-time.

The proportion of overseas students at the College has remained roughly constant in recent years. During the year under review three-quarters of our overseas students were concentrated in only two courses – studying either a Degree in Engineering or for the professional examinations of the Royal Institute of Chartered Surveyors. It has for some time been national policy that we should extend the resources of our Universities and Technical Colleges to students from overseas who have the qualifications for entry to our courses; the demands for trained men and women in developing countries are so urgent and pressing that we must play our part in meeting them. It is a very pleasant incidental result of this policy that we are able to welcome into our College community such a wide diversity of overseas students; they make a lively and characteristic contribution to

student life and we should be poorer without them.
(SWETC, 1964)

However, at South East Essex Technical College there was
an 'agreement' in 1963 to restrict the admission of full-time
and sandwich foreign students to a maximum of 15 per
cent of departmental enrolments (SEETC, 1963).

Moreover, regardless of the policies of the 1956 White
Paper to concentrate advanced work and establish a hierarchy, the growth of 'free trade' deals between LEAs and
subsequently the establishment of the 'advanced further
education pool' for funding advanced further education
enabled students from all parts of the country to select
an institution without paying higher 'out-county' fees.
The mobility of students was also supported by the
system of student grants introduced in 1962. Thus in
the 1960s the administrative geography of local authority
boundaries ceased to have much influence on students'
selection of institutions of higher education, and the
colleges increasingly saw themselves as attracting students
both nationally and internationally. The object of serving
local students seemed to have become out-dated.

CHAPTER 5
Values, Quality and Qualifications

In the course of its history, the University of East London has found itself in different parts of the higher education 'system'. From its earliest days it was linked to the universities: the staff of the West Ham college were 'recognised' by the University of London, and the college was thus able to offer London's 'internal' degrees. It was also part of a system of technical and further education maintained by local authorities. It remained in this 'public sector' of higher education throughout the years of the 'binary' policy from 1966 to 1992. Thereafter it joined the expanded 'unitary' system of higher education as a full university.

These different arrangements reflected more than a mere administrative classification: they were the institutional manifestations of different traditions of higher education. It is important to set out the main features of these traditions in order to understand the significance of the history of the University of East London.

In the course of continuing studies in higher education both in Britain and elsewhere, the present authors have described and analysed both the traditions themselves and their institutional expression (eg. Burgess and Pratt, 1970; Pratt and Burgess, 1974; Burgess, 1977; Locke, Pratt and

Burgess, 1985). Found not only in Britain but the world over, there have been the contrasting traditions of the 'autonomous' and the 'service'. The first sees higher education as an activity with its own values and purposes, affecting the rest of society obliquely and as a kind of bonus. The second explicitly expects higher education to serve individuals and society and justifies it in these terms.

The autonomous tradition can be characterised as aloof, academic, conservative and exclusive. People and institutions acting in this tradition and with this view of their purpose think it right to hold themselves apart, ready if necessary to resist the demands of society, the whims of government, the fashions of public opinion, the importunities of actual or potential students. In totalitarian countries their stand may be heroic: educational institutions are among the first to be attacked by tyrannical governments. Even in democracies, governments can err, popular demand may be misguided: both can be arbitrary, unjust and capricious. There can be no certainty where human knowledge and understanding will next be advanced, and the creations of the human mind themselves achieve a kind of autonomy, imposing their own disciplines and creating their own problems. Those people devoted to following the disciplines and solving the problems require protection from governments and social forces, to pursue free inquiry and preserve bodies of knowledge.

This characteristic of aloofness is often expressed in academic attitudes, which emphasise the preservation, extension and dissemination of knowledge, 'for its own sake'. Academics speak of pursuing truth or excellence (Jaspers, 1965) and derive their justification from a discipline or body of knowledge. They claim to spend half their academic time on research (Halsey, 1992), and claim this as essential to their teaching. The autonomous tradition does not easily accommodate specific professional or vocational training.

The tradition is educationally conservative: it resists new disciplines. Science, technology and art have all had their battles for recognition as disciplines (Roderick, 1967). It has been hard to get new matter into undergraduate courses or to drop old matter, changing the 'academic map' even harder (Perkin, 1969). This conservatism is defensible. It derives from the conviction that knowledge advances painfully by imposing order where previously there was chaos. Intellectual order is thus precious and vulnerable. Neglect of this may simply involve attempts to teach chaos.

There is an important consequence of this for students. Institutions in the autonomous tradition have to be exclusive. Given that what they do is self justifying, they can responsibly accept only those who are suitable for what they are doing. This effectively excludes most people. It is widely recognised that exclusiveness, though ostensibly academic, may be effectively social (Robbins, 1963), with middle class people overrepresented in higher education, and working class people underrepresented.

By contrast the service tradition can be characterised as responsive, vocational, innovating and open. Institutions in this tradition do not think it right to hold themselves apart from society: rather that they should respond to its needs. They seek to place the knowledge they have at the service of society. Indeed they believe that human knowledge advances as much through the solution of practical problems as through pure thought. In thus seeking to serve the tradition faces serious difficulties. In the first place there is the question of service to whom? Is it the student who is to be served, society as a whole, the government? There are many different interests: which is to be paramount? Can the institution serve more than one? The autonomous tradition settles this by asserting the priority of the discipline. The service tradition faces

human and political arguments. Clearly different interests
are not always compatible. For example, the interest of
an employer in education may be to see that his workers
should do their jobs better; the interest of the employee, by
contrast, may be to get a better job. Neither may be aware
of what society, as interpreted by an elected government,
may require or want.

Second, one of the services which educational institutions should render to a society is a serious and direct
criticism of it. But criticism is vital to a democratic
society, and a service institution is failing if it does not
offer it, though it may seem to be 'biting the hand that
feeds it'. This raises the question of accountability, and
the challenge is to work out forms of government which
will enable institutions to do their work while responding
to the society around them.

The service tradition does not, on the whole, claim to
pursue knowledge for its own sake. Its institutions are
engaged explicitly in professional and vocational education
often described as 'mere' vocational training. They attract
resources because there are actual or potential students
to be enrolled. Their 'research' is typically directed to
some external problem, often in the form of consultancy for companies. Apart from this they are typically
teaching institutions, devoted to helping students toward
some qualification. This requires them to be educationally
innovating, so they must accommodate growth, must
accept new kinds of students, offer them new kinds of
courses, create new structures of study, pioneer new forms
of governance, recruit new kinds of staff, and so on.

The service tradition means that institutions have to be
open. They cannot exclude students on the grounds that
the latter are not properly prepared. Typically they accept
'maturity' or 'experience' as an alternative to academic
qualification as an entry requirement. Their students are as
a consequence diverse; they follow courses at many levels

and by many different modes of study. Service institutions are often the traditional route to high qualification for classes excluded by the autonomous.

Although it is possible to characterise these two traditions in higher education, it is important to emphasise that they are not neatly reflected in two separate kinds of institutions. They are found in varying degrees in institutions of all kinds. The difference between them exists everywhere and is felt within institutions.

Higher education in Britain is unusual in that the existence of these two traditions has been recognized and supported by separate administrative arrangements. The universities, broadly representing the autonomous tradition, had quite different funding arrangements from other institutions. Their autonomy was and is enshrined in their individual charters. Until 1989, Government funds were distributed to universities by a committee, the University Grants Committee, whose decisions about the distribution of funds were unquestioned by Government. These allocations were made on a 'block grant' principle: that is, whatever arguments individual universities had made for the level of the grant, the actual grant, when it came, was not earmarked for specific purposes. The object of all this was to establish the UGC as a 'buffer' between the state and individual universities, thus preserving and enhancing their autonomy.

Institutions in the service tradition had quite different arrangements. Technical education since 1889 was a responsibility of local education authorities. By the 1960s there were some 700 major institutions of 'further education': technical and other colleges provided and run by public authorities. They were not protected by charters and they were administered by the same local authorities that maintained schools, under regulations made by the Secretary of State for Education and Science. Their very administration encouraged a response to demand. Courses were run and attracted resources provided it could be shown that the students were enrolled or were likely to be, or that there was an expressed need from local industry or commerce. When the numbers of qualified applicants for full time higher education exceeded those projected by the Robbins Committee (Robbins, 1963), it was the further education colleges which took them in. These arrangements for control by democratic central and local government and for public accountability offered the colleges a quite different context in which to operate from that of the universities, and this had important consequences for their actual work and their development (see Chapter 6).

However, in Britain as elsewhere there has been a tendency for institutions established in the service tradition to seek autonomy. We have called the process 'academic drift' (Pratt and Burgess, 1974). Broadly it consists of the aspiration to take on the attributes and objectives of autonomy. Non-university colleges seek freedom from public control and from the discipline of external validation. They establish the structure of subject departments and hanker after professorships. They increase their commitment to research. They try to become as much like autonomous institutions as possible, thus eschewing innovation. Most important, they may begin to reject students they would previously have accepted and they transfer elsewhere many of the courses they previously offered. The consequence is that their student body becomes increasingly homo- geneous, favouring 18 to 21 year olds from middle-class backgrounds.

The University of East London has at times in its history embraced both the traditions described here and has both accepted and resisted academic drift. Subsequent chapters will illustrate this in terms of values, policy, student intake, range of work and relations with its localities. We turn immediately, however, to the issue of qualifications.

AUTONOMY AND DEPENDENCE

It is an oddity of higher education that the many books about its aims and purposes scarcely refer to its externally most visible activity, the awarding of qualifications. Newman wrote of the university in terms of a liberal education which 'makes... the gentleman' rather than the graduate (Newman, 1873). Attending the institution was what mattered, not the gaining of a qualification. Jaspers (1965, p19) described the university as 'a community of scholars and students engaged in the task of seeking truth'. His text, written as a defence of academic freedom as the second world war came to an end, took for granted the capacity to establish the standards of that community and its scholarship, though it did discuss the need for selection and examination.

More recently, the contribution of higher education to 'certification' has been more explicitly acknowledged. The Robbins Committee stated as its first aim of higher education 'instruction of skills to play a part in the general division of labour', citing Confucius, no less, in support. It spoke of skills which demanded special training, implicitly acknowledging the need for their certification (Robbins, 1963, p6).

Once the issue of qualification is addressed, a host of questions arise. Who is to establish the standards? How are they to be enforced? How are courses to be structured? What qualifications are appropriate for what achievements? Are there different levels of courses? What should be the content of courses, and who should decide that? and so on. Any institution aspiring to offer higher education finds itself facing these kind of questions. The University of East London and its constituent colleges both faced them and offered a variety of answers. It may even be said to be reverting now to the answers rejected at the time of its designation as a polytechnic twenty years earlier.

The two traditions of higher education described above

have differently influenced the arrangements made to determine and control the structure and content of courses and the standards of qualifications. Institutions in the autonomous tradition have been substantially free to create their own courses and syllabuses, to examine their own students and to award their own qualifications. A university's powers to do this are, mostly, enshrined in Royal Charters. The senate is the principal academic body, responsible for academic policy and teaching, examinations and discipline. Staff and departments wishing to create or amend courses generally do so without having to meet formal requirements of bodies outside the senate. (There are exceptions to this in subjects where professional bodies control admission to particular professions, though in the end the university still has the power to create courses and award degrees in these subjects, whether or not the professional body chooses to recognise them.)

Institutions in the service tradition have, historically, not had these powers. They could and did create courses and award qualifications – but these qualifications carried little external recognition or currency, such as inhere in university degrees. The solutions to this problem of recognition have been various and the effects diverse.

In the early years of our colleges, particularly at West Ham, the majority of students were on courses that led to the colleges' own qualifications and to awards of professional and examining bodies. The records of the colleges themselves, reflecting their academic ambitions, often give pride of place to their degree level work. Yet for most of their existence, the bulk of the colleges' work was on these other courses, in response to demand from local students and their employers.

The early prospectuses of the West Ham college show that certificates were awarded by the Council to students completing at least three years of study including both theoretical and practical work. Board of Education certificates were available for certain levels of attainment in science and arts courses.

But gradually, the College developed courses leading to other awards and its own Certificates diminished in importance. Even so college certificates and diplomas remained an important part of the range of qualifications offered by the institutions, up to and after their amalgamation into the North East London Polytechnic.

The Essex colleges equally offered a wide range of courses. By the time of their foundations, the earlier practice of offering mainly college certificates had been superseded by external qualifications, so the bulk of the colleges' syllabuses were mainly determined elsewhere.

To attain recognition for the courses and qualifications, the institutions had to teach to syllabuses created by external bodies, which have examined students and awarded qualifications. One of the most 'unequal' (Venables, 1955) versions of this relationship was in arrangements for external degrees of some universities (mainly the University of London) to be offered in technical colleges. A technical college in the first half of this century typically found itself teaching students on engineering courses created by the University senate (on which it would not have members), for examinations approved by the senate, for qualifications of the university.

Colleges wishing to submit candidates for external degrees of London University had, from the 1930s on, to be inspected by the University. By the early 1950s, more than 30 colleges had met the University's requirements and over 1,100 external degrees were awarded to students in technical colleges. The constituent colleges of the future University of East London were amongst these. The technical colleges disliked this subordinate relationship. Venables criticised the University for bringing in changes with only 'a semblance of consultation by way of invited comments on paper'. But he recognised its importance as a route to graduate status for many thousands of students.

Another unequal relationship for the technical colleges (and other institutions including the universities) was that with the professional institutions. These autonomous bodies set requirements for membership and professional recognition. Many are statutory bodies so that it is not possible to practise in their field without their recognition. Different institutions have different practices: some set and mark their own examinations; many accept existing qualifications, such as degrees, as wholly or partly exempting students from their requirements.

Venables records that the professional institutions 'exercised a profound influence on the growth and orientation of technical education.' Their prescription of standards, syllabus and the conduct of examinations meant that colleges had 'very little academic autonomy'. However, some institutions did involve the colleges in aspects of partnership through representation on education and examination committees. Others recognised colleges, after inspection, as suitable for offering the institution's examination.

PARTNERSHIPS

Technical colleges did benefit from a range of more equal arrangements involving external agencies, described by Venables as 'partnerships' (Venables, 1955). Indeed these partnerships became a major characteristic of institutions in the service tradition sector, and eventually characterised one of the most potent influences on higher education this century, the Council for National Academic Awards.

One of these partnerships was with the universities, particularly the University of London, which enabled some London colleges to teach students on internal rather than external degrees of the University. Colleges in the London area were eligible for this status, and were able to have qualified staff as 'recognised teachers' of the University.

Seven colleges achieved this status, and the West Ham college was one of these from its establishment.

But for many colleges founded at the time of our precursor institutions, university links were a minor part of their work, if they figured at all. From very early in the history of technical education, examining bodies were founded which offered a national framework for qualifications. There was a large number of such bodies, offering qualifications which would now be classified as in 'further education', and many of them still exist.

These examining bodies were mostly founded in the mid nineteenth century in response to the current concern about technical education. Typically they had representation of colleges, as well as other educational institutions and professions. One of the oldest was the Union of Lancashire and Cheshire Institutes (UCLI), founded in 1839, and stemming directly from the mechanics' institutes (Venables, 1955). By the 1950s, the regional unions were 'effective federations or partnerships of local education authorities and educational institutions' (Venables, 1955, p147). In the 1950s UCLI had over 50,000 students pursuing its courses. Other regional examining unions followed. In 1880, the livery companies of London established the City and Guilds of London Institute (CGLI), whose courses became a mainstay of the education of many technicians and are still widely available. In the 1950s, over 80,000 candidates entered for its examinations. The Royal Society of Arts (RSA) was another body which had established examinations in the nineteenth century and was still making a major contribution to further education, mainly in commercial subjects, and higher education.

The most important, historically and educationally, of the partnerships was that for the system of National Certificates and Diplomas. The system evolved in 1921 to meet the need for a high level qualification for part time study. The various examining bodies offered a range of qualifications and an incentive to continued study in many crafts and trades at what is now mainly FE level. Venables records that to fill the gap at the higher levels, the Board of Education discussed with the Institution of Mechanical Engineers the creation of a qualification 'approaching the standard of a degree for engineers through part time study' and in a way that would permit 'reasonable freedom and flexibility in teaching method'.

Venables notes that 1921 was thus 'a notable date in the history and development of technical education'. The scheme was launched that year in mechanical engineering and in chemistry, and these were followed by other subjects. Two levels were offered: Ordinary (held to be roughly comparable, later, with GCE A level) and Higher (gained by two years of part time study after ONC). Full time diploma courses were also established. The scheme was the backbone of work for many colleges and the HNC was the first step of the ladder of higher education for many part time students, and their colleges. By 1953 over 22,000 candidates entered Certificate examinations at Ordinary level and over 9,000 for HNC. For OND and HND the numbers were in the hundreds.

The schemes initiated a system of partnership that was to characterise technical education and later higher education outside the universities. The scheme was run by National Committees, composed of representatives of the education Ministries (of England and Wales, Scotland and Northern Ireland) and the relevant professional institutions (sometimes more than one). Later representatives of the colleges were involved, too.

The benefit of the scheme for a college was the national currency given to its own initiative, typically in response to local industrial needs. The college would discuss its proposal with HMI, design it within the rules and apply for approval to the joint committee. For the student, the same national currency meant they were often exempted